# Coming Clean

*How to Confront and Confess Your Mistakes and Move On*

Anthony Q. Knotts

Kingdom Publishing, LLC
1350 Blair Drive
Odenton, MD 21113
www.kingdompublishingllc.com

Printed in the United States of America

Coming Clean
How to Confront and Confess Your Mistakes and Move On

Copyright © 2017 by Anthony Q. Knotts

All rights reserved. No part of this book may be reproduced, stored in a retrieval system, or transmitted in any form or by any means without written permission of the author.

Unless otherwise indicated, Scripture quotations are taken from the King James Version of the Holy Bible, 1995, Zondervan Corporation, and the Holy Bible, New International Version, Copyright © 1973, 1978, 1984 by the International Bible Society. Used by permission of Zondervan Publishing House. The "NIV" and "New International Version" trademarks are registered in the United States Patent and Trademark Office by the International Bible Society. New King James Version (NKJV) Copyright © 1979, 1980, 1982, by Thomas Nelson, Inc. Used by permission. All rights reserved.

ISBN 978-0-9982100-9-4

Library of Congress Control Number: 2017948981

Because of the dynamic nature of the Internet, any web addresses or links contained in this book may have changed since publication and may no longer be valid. The views expressed in this work are solely those of the author and do not necessarily reflect the views of the publisher, and the publisher hereby disclaims any responsibility for them.

## Acknowledgements

First and foremost, I would like to thank God for His plan of repentance, Jesus Christ for paying the price for me to be able to repent, and Holy Spirit for His abiding presence that convicts me to embrace this precious gift of repentance.

I would like to thank my beautiful wife, Byrdie, for always being supportive of all the things I do. I want to thank my children, Teland, Jalen and Destiny for sharing me with the world.

I also thank my Embassy Church sons and daughters past, present and future.

Last but not least, I thank Jacenta Cobb, Latasha Moore and Melanie Jones for assistance in making the revelation on repentance a reality.

This Book is dedicated to Jacenta Cobb for believing this could be a book when it was only on CD and the effort you put in to take it from Logos to Rhema!

## *Table of Contents*

*Introduction*
1

CHAPTER ONE
*A New Perspective of Repentance*
7

CHAPTER TWO
*The Privilege of Repentance*
25

CHAPTER THREE
*The Power of Repentance*
33

CHAPTER FOUR
*The Purpose of Repentance*
39

CHAPTER FIVE
*The Process of Repentance*
57

CHAPTER SIX
*The Prize of Repentance*
89

CHAPTER SEVEN
*Peter's Take on Repentance*
93

# *Introduction*

It has been 25 years now, and I can vividly remember the encounter that led me to give my life to Christ. Shortly after drinking repulsively and indulging in illicit sexual activity, I had a divine encounter with the Holy Spirit. He came into my hotel room and impacted my life; so much so that I found myself standing at the altar at New Faith Baptist Church asking Jesus Christ to cleanse me of my sins and to save my wretched soul. Coming facing to face with sin in my life left me with a broken and contrite spirit. But I found a new beginning in life as I took advantage of the opportunity to "Come Clean."

> *Repentance is siding with God against self.*
> *– Todd Nibert*

The first words spoken by Jesus Christ, as recorded in the New Testament, are "Repent ... for the kingdom of heaven is at hand" (Matt. 3:2). Repentance is a divine principle and is required for man's salvation into the kingdom of heaven.

Todd Nibert said, "Repentance is siding with God against self."[1]

When we accept Christ as our Lord and personal Savior, there is an *initial* repentance that saves us from the eternal penalty of sin. But as we grow in our walk with Him, repentance should become a part of our daily prayer life and communication with God.

Repentance and trust in Christ's redeeming blood result in total remission of sin, and that means pardon, forgiveness, and freedom from the power of sin. According to Scripture, there can be no conversion, no freedom, and no born-again miracle without repentance:

> *According to Scripture, there can be no conversion, no freedom, and no born-again miracle without repentance.*

"Repent ye therefore, and be converted, that your sins may be blotted out, when the times of refreshing shall come from the presence of the Lord" (Acts 3:19).

David O. McKay when speaking on the importance of repentance, said, "Every principle and ordinance of the gospel of Jesus Christ is significant and important in contributing to the progress, happiness, and eternal life of man, but there is none more essential to the salvation of the human family than the divine and eternally operative

---

[1] Todd Nibert, Quotes on Repentance, www.goodread.com

## Introduction

principle, repentance. Without it, no one can be saved. Without it, no one can ... progress."[2]

Satan is strongly against any man repenting and preparing himself for the kingdom of heaven. Satan's mission and goal is to destroy man's potential godliness and his preparation to be one again with his Heavenly Father. Repentance will stop the devil and keep him from entering the hearts of men. Once a person "Comes Clean" through the gift of repentance, there is no more distance between him and his heavenly Father.

Thomas Watson, Sr. defines repentance as, "A grace of God whereby a person is inwardly humbled and visibly transformed."[3] Repentance is how God put the human race back in His grace. Real Christ followers are marked by repentance, not just at conversion, but every day for the rest of their lives.

The Bible makes it very clear that in the last days most people will not repent. In fact, during the Great Tribulation people will obviously be under the direct, material, tangible, fierce judgment of God but they will not repent. Preaching a no change, low commitment, me-centered Christianity will not produce the kind of conviction that will cause people to "Come Clean" and repent. Rather, it produces large crowds and can fill up arenas with people looking to have a good

---

[2] David O. McKay, Gospel Ideals, Improvements Era, 1953, p. 13
[3] Thomas Watson, Sr. , www.todaysbiblestudy.com

time but not looking to have a life changing experience with God. Revelation 9:20 says, "The rest of mankind, who were not killed by these plagues, did not repent of the works of their hands nor give up worshiping demons and idols of gold and silver and bronze and stone and wood, which cannot see or hear or walk, nor did they repent of their murders or their sorceries or their sexual immorality or their thefts."

Repentance is not meritorious. Only the sacrifice of Christ's blood can forgive. Repentance is the only way to know true healing and rejoicing. There is no other way to enter the peace and rest of Christ except through the doors of repentance. Dieter F. Uchtdorf said, "The heavens will not be filled with those who never made mistakes but with those who recognized that they were off course and who corrected their ways to get back in the light of gospel truth."[4] Paul wrote to the Corinthians about the fruit that results from repentance when he said, "Godly sorrow worketh repentance to salvation not to be repented of: but the sorrow of the world worketh death. For behold this selfsame thing, that ye sorrowed after a godly sort, what carefulness it wrought in you, yea, what clearing of yourselves, yea, what indignation, yea, what fear" (2 Corinthians 7:10–11).

Repentance is the renewal of life. This means we must free ourselves from all our negative traits and turn toward

---

[4] Dieter F. Uctdorf, Quotes on Repentance, www.goodreads.com

## Introduction

absolute good.  No sin is unforgivable except the sin of unrepentance.  That Sunday morning twenty-five years ago, I personally discovered the freedom that repentance provides when you "Come Clean."  Coming clean that Sunday morning led to me being forgiven — and that forgiveness produced rest and rejoicing in my heart.  I pray that as you read this book you will have an open heart to embrace a revelation on something that we hear little about today in our churches.  This same revelation that I'm sharing with you in this book has made a big difference in my life.  I pray that you, too, will COME CLEAN!

CHAPTER ONE

# A New Perspective of Repentance

When I accepted Jesus Christ as my Lord and Savior, I joined the church but there was no immediate external change in my behavior. However, the more I began to read and study the Bible and the more I exposed myself to different teachings, I started to realize that my lifestyle, behavior, and mindset would have to change. Repentance was the only way this change could be achieved.

Before I gained a thorough understanding of repentance and its application in my life, church seemed more like a country club than the Kingdom of God being manifested on Earth. For years whenever I heard the word *repent* (or *repentance*) in the church it was used with a negative connotation. It made me believe the concept of repentance was not being shared in the way that God had originally designed for His people. I wrote this book based upon the desire to share a perspective about repentance that God imparted into me.

Before I began writing this book, I decided to study the word repent. I found out that there are three (3) simple meanings for repentance. They are:

1. To be sorry, have a feeling of remorse;
2. To turn from sin and dedicate oneself to the amendment of one's life and
3. To prepare or make ready.

Let's briefly elaborate on each definition of repentance.

## Repent – First Definition
### *To be sorry, have a feeling of remorse*

The Bible mentions in 2 Corinthians 7:10 that "For godly sorrow worketh repentance to salvation not to be repented of…" When we operate in the biblical principle of repentance we recognize our wrong and are truly remorseful. It's important to note that there is a difference between *regret* and *remorse*. Regret can be defined as to be sorry or disappointed over something that has happened or been done, while remorse is considered a deep guilt for a wrong committed. Regret can exist without remorse. For instance, we can feel sorry about something and regret that it ever happened but be completely void of any feeling of remorse.

## Chapter One - A New Perspective of Repentance

On the other hand, we can acknowledge guilt – and to some degree consider how others might judge us – but our conviction is not strong enough to stop us from doing the same thing repeatedly. This leads us to the second definition of the word *repent*.

<u>Repent – Second Definition</u>
***To turn from sin and dedicate oneself to the amendment of one's life***

When we have remorse or a true godly sorrow, it leads us to actively turn away from wrong behavior. Practicing repentance can have a major impact on our spiritual relationship with God as well as the relationships we have with others. We tend to develop behavioral characteristics based upon our actions and it eventually influences how we view ourselves.

Let's take a look at King David's sin. He seduced Bathsheba knowing that she was a married woman. His behavior not only affected his relationship with God, but it also affected Bathsheba's husband, Uriah who was a warrior in King David's army. Uriah was left abandoned to die at the hands of his enemies. God was not pleased with King David's sin and therefore expressed His reproach which ultimately

> *When we have remorse or a true godly sorrow, it leads us to actively turn away from wrong behavior.*

caused King David to repent for the deceitful thing he had done. Once we see the effect of our decisions, repentance gives us the ability to make a U-turn and go in another direction. Let's move to the third definition which epitomizes my new perspective on repentance.

<u>Repent – Third Definition</u>
***To prepare or make ready***

This particular meaning completes the process of repentance. First, we have remorse, then we turn away from sin and return to God, and now we are ready for whatever He has in store for us.

    Typically, when born again believers make their initial confession of faith and give their lives to Christ, a church clergyman hands them a copy of the Bible which is often viewed as a thick book of rules. This is the old perspective. However, I think the new perspective of repentance has a more positive spin on Kingdom purpose. Through this new perspective of repentance we are instructed on what to do and how to act instead of merely receiving a comprehensive list of all of the things the Bible says we should not do.

    When we repent, we are letting God know that we are ready. Maybe you're wondering what exactly you are ready for. Repentance makes us ready for the blessings God has in store for us. After going through the process, we should be ready to do whatever God asks and requires of us.

## Chapter One - A New Perspective of Repentance

I need to emphasize a major point. True biblical repentance involves the heart – leave your head out of it.

Hosea 10:12 says, "Sow to yourselves in righteousness, reap in mercy; break up your fallow ground: for it is time to seek the Lord, till He come and rain righteousness upon you." This is a powerful Scripture. I believe this verse tells us to break up the fallow ground of our *heart*. This Biblical context discusses how God is speaking to Israel, a country that relies strongly on agriculture. Farming is how a majority of the people earned a living. So God uses a metaphor the people of Israel can easily understand. You can ask any farmer about planting seeds and they will tell you that before you plant a seed you must first till the ground. The purpose for tilling the ground is to soften the soil. The soil must be soft in order for the seed to adequately be planted for potential growth.

> *It is impossible to reap a harvest if the seeds are not planted on fertile ground.*

Farmers use plows to break up the ground before planting crops. The whole intent for tilling the ground and planting the seed is to *reap a harvest*. It is impossible to reap a harvest if the seeds are not planted on fertile ground.

Upon further examination of the Hosea 10 farming analogy, we can see how it applies to our lives today. God represents the farmer and our hearts are symbolic of the ground. In order for God to reap a harvest in our lives, He has to first plant a seed in our hearts. It is absolutely impossible for Him to plant seeds in the untilled and unbroken soil of a hard heart. This is where repentance comes into play. It's God's way of breaking up the fallow ground of our hearts. He turns our hearts over to Him. Thus, when we repent, we make a confession that we want our hearts to be ready.

Another powerful point about repentance is that it prepares us for the return of Christ. For years, people have been spreading the message, "Jesus is on His way back!" In fact, this very same message is still being shared today. The phenomenon of Christ's return was first pronounced in the book of Genesis. Remember when Adam sinned? As a result, God said that Satan would bruise the heel of the seed of the woman, but he (the seed of the woman) would crush Satan's head. Prophetically, this is the first reference to Jesus Christ's descent to Earth. From Genesis 3:15 to Malachi, we read of several prophecies that predict Jesus' arrival on Earth. We know Christ's initial purpose was to offer salvation and redemption to the lost sheep of Israel, the Jews. However, the Gentiles would also benefit from Jesus. On the day of His return, the Bible tells us that all who believe in Christ, both Jews and Gentiles, will be reconciled back to the Father.

According to the prophecies, people who lived during the B.C. era knew that the Messiah (Christ) was coming. Yet, when He showed up, a lot of them still were not ready to receive and accept Jesus of Nazareth for who He was – the Messiah. Even today we are living under that same prophecy

## Chapter One - A New Perspective of Repentance

– Jesus is coming. Unfortunately, doubt clouds the validity of this claim. Realistically, if Jesus was to show up today, many people inside and outside of the church would not be ready. Why not, since the Bible tells us He would come?

Isaiah 7:14 states, "Therefore the Lord himself shall give you a sign; behold a virgin shall conceive, and bear a son, and shall call his name Immanuel." In Malachi 3, the new perspective of repentance is discussed. Malachi 3:1 says, "Behold, I will send my messenger, and he shall prepare the way for me: and the Lord, whom ye seek, shall suddenly come to his temple, even the messenger of the covenant, whom ye delight in: behold, he shall come, saith the Lord of hosts."

We must also embrace the ministry of John the Baptist if we are going to embrace the ministry of Jesus Christ. You cannot have one without the other. Under this new perspective, John the Baptist is synonymous with repentance. The word "repent" can be substituted for John's name whenever you are reading the Bible. For instance, the Malachi 3:1 is a Scripture prophesying the existence of John the Baptist. This prophecy is something we can see on the surface. But if you dig deeper, you will see John the Baptist is the *spirit of repentance*. The Scripture is basically saying that God is going to send the spirit of repentance and when it arrives, the Lord will come to His temple. We are God's temple and the Holy Ghost is supposed to live in us.

## Coming Clean

In Exodus, God told Moses to build Him a sanctuary that He might dwell amongst the people. Once the sanctuary, a mobile temple, was finished, the glory of the Lord appeared. God's ultimate goal is to dwell among His people. This is possible when we invite the Holy Spirit into our hearts. Repentance is what gets us ready for the infilling of the Holy Spirit.

When speaking of the infilling of the Holy Spirit I must highlight Pentecost. It was at that time that the disciples were all filled with the Holy Spirit. BUT there could never have been a Pentecost without a Passover. Pentecost deals with outpouring of the Spirit while Passover deals with the shedding of blood.

> *Without repentance Christ cannot enter our hearts. We cannot be filled with the Holy Spirit apart from repentance.*

Repentance allows us to apply the blood of Jesus to ourselves, our situations and our circumstances. When we repent it is like taking a blood bath. The more I repent, the more the Lord gains access into my life. If you notice, none of this can take place until the *messenger* arrives. That messenger is John the Baptist. His ministry must come first because he has to *prepare the way*.

Without repentance Christ cannot enter our hearts. The more I repent, the more He can come into my life. When this happens, God, through the Holy Spirit, will begin to expose areas in your life where deception and darkness exist; the

## Chapter One - A New Perspective of Repentance

very areas where Satan has dominion. God discloses to us our darkest sins and shines a light on us that we may rid them from our lives. If we confess our sins, He is faithful and just to forgive, cleanse and restore us (1 John 1:9).

When we make a heartfelt confession of our sins before God, He will show us our sins. The moment we repent we are then cleansed from our sins and free to move forward. The result of repentance is that we are essentially making room for Christ, the Anointed One, and His anointing to show up in our lives. This cannot take place without repentance.

The old and most widely accepted perspective of repentance is associated with guilt, namely because we are made to feel like we have disappointed God. In retrospect, repentance is in fact a joyful word. It is, after all, what allows us to regain oneness, fellowship and intimacy with the Almighty. The more we repent to God, the more we are really saying, "God, I'm sorry. Yes, I will return to you." Basically, we take full responsibility for living independent of Him and now we are taking the initiative to restore a right relationship with God. By repenting we acknowledge our readiness for Christ to come into our lives.

> By repenting we acknowledge our readiness for Christ to come into our lives.

Once we experience true repentance our behavior changes. Regardless of what happened in the past we are no longer at liberty to hold onto grudges or painful memories.

Repentance teaches us the importance of getting past the place where we refuse to forgive others. As long as we walk around unwilling to forgive and unwilling to repent, we actually cause Christ to lift and leave. Ezekiel 8 and 9 tells us about how the presence of the Lord lifted and went to the Mount of Olives because of the abominations going on inside the temple. The sins of the people of Israel and their unwillingness to repent caused God's presence to leave.

Remember, the enemy doesn't want us to repent. He knows that sin makes us candidates for destruction. This fact alone should give us enough motivation to repent because we know that when we do, we open our hearts to Christ. Malachi 3:2 reads, "But who may abide the day of his coming? And who shall stand when he appeareth? For he is like a refiner's fire, and like fuller's soap." This Scripture suggests that if you haven't embraced the ministry of John the Baptist (the first messenger), when Jesus Christ comes you will fall under judgment. The verse continues, "And he shall sit as a refiner and a purifier of silver: and he shall purify the sons of Levi and purge them as gold and silver that they may offer unto the Lord an offering in righteousness."

When we accept the ministry of John the Baptist which is also the new perspective of repentance, it refines and purifies our minds, hearts and actions. The old perspective does nothing more than put emphasis on what we have done wrong. Whereas the new perspective allows us to

## Chapter One - A New Perspective of Repentance

concentrate on what we are about to do and that it is right according to the standards of Christ.

I've written this book to effectively expose the enemy and his deceitful schemes and empower every reader with the necessary tools to defeat Satan once and for all. The body of Christ needs a spiritual cleansing to get rid of all our sinful buildup. Repentance is the first step.

Malachi 3:4 says, "Then shall the offering of Judah and Jerusalem be pleasant unto the Lord, as in the days of old, and as in former years." Here God says that He is willing to accept their offering. The spirit of repentance makes what we offer to God acceptable in His sight. Verse 5 reads, "And I will come near to you to judgment; and I will be a swift witness against the sorcerers, and against the adulterers, and against false swearers and against those that oppress the hirelings in his wages, the widow, and the fatherless, and that turn aside the stranger from his right, and fear not me, saith the Lord of hosts." Since the people repented, God says that He is back on their side as long as they steer clear of the aforementioned things and continue to fear the Lord their God.

Based upon this passage of Scripture, there are three points to take note of. When the spirit of repentance or the ministry of John the Baptist takes place, it causes a behavior change. Real biblical repentance changes our behavior because we start to modify our decisions to avoid making the same mistakes over and over again. In most cases, repentance can bring about a lifestyle change as well.

Repentance also changes *God's* behavior. This Scripture reveals how God was ready to bring judgment because the people are living in sin. This means Satan, the deceiver, is sitting back pleased with his work; he's happy with the fact that God's people will be judged. When we repent, however, we may be chastened by God but will not be judged the same way God will judge the world of unbelievers (1 Corinthians 11:32). When we repent, we may have to shoulder some pain or suffer loss, but we will not be condemned with the world. Repentance also changes *Satan's* behavior. He comes to steal, kill and destroy but when we repent and change our behavior, it changes how Satan behaves as well. He no longer has a right to destroy us. Through repentance we restore our inheritance of God's blessing instead of allowing Satan to carry out judgment on us.

> *We should look for reasons to repent, not reasons to sin.*

The irony is that we should be looking for reasons to repent, not reasons to sin. The more I repent, the more I open myself up for Christ to come into His temple. I am His temple! Sadly, some of us choose to walk around with an excess of sin in our hearts. This is why God can look at our hearts and see sin instead of His own reflection.

## Chapter One - A New Perspective of Repentance

Malachi says that if we follow John (the spirit of repentance) we will be introduced to a messenger who will act as a *refiner* and a *purifier*. What repentance does is introduce us to the cleansing power of Jesus' blood that we may began to purify ourselves from our old, sinful ways. Once this process occurs, then God can look at us and see Himself. It's funny how some people can get an attitude and feel like, "I am not going to repent because this is how I am." Yet, it is important to understand that when God looks down upon us, our flesh cannot glory in His presence. Our very existence should be to glorify God in spirit and in truth.

Even in the New Testament, repentance comes before *redemption*. In Matthew 3: 1-2 we find, "In those days came John the Baptist, preaching in the wilderness of Judea, And saying, <u>Repent ye</u>: for the kingdom of heaven is at hand." John is still saying the same thing today. The spirit of John is telling us to repent because repentance gets us ready for the kingdom. Luke 12: 32 says, "It is the Father's good pleasure to give you the kingdom." It can be acquired when we're willing to submit to John's ministry of repentance.

Matthew 3:3 tells us, "For this is he that was spoken of by Esaias, saying, The voice of one crying in the wilderness, *prepare* ye the way of the Lord, make his paths straight." The word *prepare* means *to make ready*. Look at what happens here – John tells the people to *prepare*. Both John the Baptist and Isaiah prophesied about the coming of Jesus. The prophecy in Isaiah 40 tells us that John the Baptist would be the "voice of one crying in the wilderness" warning the people to "prepare ye the way of the Lord." In fact, the only time that Jesus comes before John is in prophecy. From the beginning, in Genesis 3:15, God pronounces that He would send Jesus Christ to the earth.

Believers today also need to heed that voice of repentance; that voice that's crying out in the wilderness, "Repent!" God wants to raise up pastors who will offer instructions on the proper way to repent and teach the true purpose of repentance. The Bible says in 2 Chronicles 7:14, "If my people who are called by my name shall humble themselves and pray and turn from their wicked ways; then will I hear from heaven, and will forgive their sins and will heal their land." This was a scriptural promise originally assigned to the children of Israel. Through the spirit of adoption which allows believers to cry out, 'Abba Father," we can also claim this promise for our lives.

The passage in Matthew 3:3 continues, "For this is He that was spoken of by the prophet Esaias, saying, The voice of one crying in the wilderness, Prepare ye the way of the Lord, make his paths straight. And the same John had his raiment of camel's hair, and a leather girdle about his loins; and his meat was locusts and wild honey." It is safe to say that John the Baptist was a strange man, not only because of his attire and diet, but because in our day some people would view repentance as a strange word.

## Chapter One - A New Perspective of Repentance

Matthew 3:5 says, "Then went out to him Jerusalem, and all Judaea, and all the region about Jordan." Did you see what happened? The church went out embracing repentance! That is what today's church has to do. We have to embrace the ministry of repentance. According to the new perspective, we have to totally accept the spirit of repentance.

In the Old Testament, when the people knew they were facing judgment they would tear their clothes, wear sackcloth, and put ashes on their face as a sign of mourning. A good example of this is when God sent Jonah to Nineveh. He told the people that their city would be overthrown in forty days. The king called a fast and the people humbled themselves with prayer and repentance. God saw their actions and spared them.

Thank God we are not called to tear our clothes. Instead, through the ministry of John the Baptist, God's calling us to rend our hearts. He wants to rain down righteousness in our lives. John's ministry is repentance and Jesus' ministry is that of righteousness (or right standing) with the Father. Jesus allows us to be declared innocent even though we could easily be found guilty.

The connection between John and Jesus is similar to soap and perfume. We use soap and water to clean our bodies of dirt and sweat. Sometimes we add a touch of cologne or perfume to compliment the way we smell. However, it would be a big mistake to use a scented fragrance in place of taking a bath. Similarly, one can never put on Jesus before they put on John. It simply will not work. If you want the presence of God to show up in your life, embrace the ministry of John because Jesus is never far away.

We've already established the fact that John is on the scene. The disciples went out to Jerusalem, Judea, and all the regions to teach the importance of accepting the ministry of Jesus Christ. According to Matthew 3:6, "And they were baptized of him in Jordan, confessing their sins." Afterwards, there was repentance. The Scripture continues: "But when he saw many of the Pharisees and Sadducees come to his baptism, he said unto them, O generation of vipers, who hath warned you to flee from the wrath to come?" God was prepared to release his wrath on Israel, but because of His great love toward us He sent John as a lifeline. In Matthew 3:8, the Bible says, "Bring forth therefore fruits meet for *repentance*." Verse 11 continues with, "I indeed baptize you with water unto *repentance*: but he that cometh after me is mightier than I, whose shoes I am not worthy to bear: he shall baptize you with the Holy Ghost, and with fire." Even though Jesus is mightier than John, we cannot devalue the importance of John the Baptist. His ministry of repentance gets us ready for Jesus' ministry, that is eternal life and the gift of the Holy Ghost. You can't get Holy Ghost and fire until

{ *When we repent we position ourselves to receive the Holy Ghost and fire.* }

## Chapter One - A New Perspective of Repentance

Jesus releases it. When we repent, we position ourselves to receive the Holy Ghost and fire.

Matthew 3:12 says, "Whose fan is in his hand, and he will thoroughly purge his floor, and gather his wheat into the garner; but he will burn up the chaff with unquenchable fire. Then cometh Jesus from Galilee to Jordan unto John, to be baptized of him." Even Jesus submitted to the ministry of John the Baptist. Just like us, Jesus Himself went through a process of fulfilling all righteousness including baptism. Jesus told John that "All righteousness had to be fulfilled." As a man, Jesus, too, had to prepare Himself to receive the Holy Spirit which descended upon Him like a dove.

> *There is one thing the enemy never wants believers to grab hold to; and that is a thorough understanding of repentance.*

The Bible tells us John was already on the scene when Jesus arrived. This lets us know that the more willing we are to practice John's ministry, the more we can experience the benefits of what Jesus has to offer. Repenting leads us to the final step of redemption.

1 Peter 5: 8 warns us to be careful and vigilant because our adversary, Satan, is like a roaring lion walking around seeking anyone he can devour. The enemy will sit back patiently and watch us shout, speak in tongues and wait our turn in the prophecy line. These are times when he doesn't see us as a threat to his kingdom. Rest assured, however,

there is one thing that the enemy never wants believers to grab hold to; and that is a thorough understanding of repentance. He's pleased with the traditional or old perspective of repentance because it is inaccurate, misleading, and leaves room for deception. The enemy's goal is for us to never gain a true revelation of the ministry of John. God, however, does things in decency and in order. He laid out a formula and the first step toward redemption is repentance.

    A lot of people want more of Jesus, but have yet to give John the Baptist a second thought. Oddly enough, their desires won't be fulfilled until they come to the realization that repentance opens the door to their desire for more of Jesus. The new perspective becomes relevant because it teaches us that indulging in the ministry of John the Baptist means opening up our hearts to Christ.

CHAPTER TWO

# The Privilege of Repentance

Based on a true lack of understanding, some of us have taken for granted what a privilege repenting really is. There are benefits to understanding and applying the ministry of John the Baptist in our Christian walk.

The main privilege is that God stamps repentance with His own guarantee. He goes the extra mile in removing sin from us, forgetting about them and then allowing us to forget about them as well.

After researching repentance in the Bible, I found some additional benefits besides the ones I just mentioned. In Matthew 3:1-2, the Bible reads: "In those days came John the Baptist, preaching in the wilderness of Judea, and saying Repent ye: for the kingdom of heaven is at hand." This concept is simple but very powerful. Repentance gets you ready for *heaven*. John said, "Repent, for the kingdom of heaven is at hand."

Another benefit can be found in Colossians 1:13. The Scripture tells us that "[God] has delivered us from the power of darkness, and hath translated us into the kingdom of his dear Son: in whom we have redemption through his blood, even the forgiveness of sin." Repentance *delivers us from the hand of the devil*. The more we repent, the more the enemy has to take his hand off our lives. In case you are wondering, the act of repentance allows you to be delivered from the bondage of Satan. However, if you do not repent, he can still have a grip on your life causing you to succumb to his deceptive plan which he crafted to keep you down.

> *Repentance gets you ready for heaven.*

I will not hesitate to repent, especially since it means the enemy will have to take his hand off my life. The Bible teaches us not to give place to the devil. Maybe you don't, but if someone else does, it can still affect you. When you repent, whether it's for your actions or the outcome of someone else's, you get *closure*. You will feel empowered to move past sinful thoughts, ungodly behavior, and painful situations from your past. On the other hand, one who is not willing to repent can never experience closure; instead they will remain without closure.

## Chapter Two - The Privilege of Repentance

When we repent, Satan has no other choice but to take his hand off of us. Why? Because whenever we ask for the Lord's forgiveness, we are confessing our sins. 1 John 1:9 says that if we confess our sins, God is faithful and just to forgive us. He will also cleanse us. The enemy has to release his hold on our lives because when we repent, the blood of Jesus is made manifest in our lives.

> *Oftentimes we do not repent from our past because we want to continue to dabble in it. We get pleasure from the things that we desperately need to let go of. Cherishing sin can make us miss heaven.*

We are cleansed by the blood of the Lamb and by the Word of God. The enemy cannot reside in a place where the blood and the Word exist.

As mentioned earlier, repentance gets us ready for heaven. It allows us to inherit the rights of a son or a daughter of God through the *Spirit of adoption*. Once a person confesses with their mouth and believes in their heart that Jesus Christ died for their sins, then they can wholeheartedly accept Jesus as their personal Savior. That intimate relationship ties us to God. This is true according to Romans 8:15-16, where we cry, "Abba Father." Your soul no longer belongs to the devil, although he'll still try and come after you like he did the children of Israel. When you repent

> *When we repent, Satan has no other choice but to take his hand off of us!*

it is as if you're walking through the Red Sea. When you put on your spiritual covering of Jesus' blood, neither Pharaoh nor the devil can pursue you because if they do they will drown.

The blood of Jesus is strong enough to drown the enemy out from your present and also from your past. In chapter 3 of the book of Philippians, Paul says, "This one thing I do; forgetting about the things that are behind me and I'm reaching forth to the things that are before me." As you're reaching forth, understand the enemy is coming after you. Be encouraged and keep going forward. Rest assured if you never outgrow repentance, the enemy will eventually be defeated.

Oftentimes we do not repent from our past because we want to continue to dabble in it. We get pleasure from the things that we desperately need to let go of. Cherishing sin can make us miss heaven. However, all is not lost even though we may still have to mature spiritually. Thank God for instituting repentance. It allows us to stop holding onto the strongholds that give the enemy just enough room to sneak in and try to attack us where we are most vulnerable.

I am certainly grateful to know repentance is truly a prize and not a surprise. Here's why: a surprise is something you do not know about until it happens. In most cases, you are not required to do anything to get a surprise. A prize, however, is something you can expect. Repentance fails to be categorized as a surprise because the Bible tells us in

## Chapter Two - The Privilege of Repentance

legible black ink what happens when we repent. There is no misunderstanding about the fact that repentance is a prize if we choose to accept it and follow the biblical process to receive it.

Acts 2:38 says, "Then Peter said unto them, Repent, and be baptized every one of you in the name of Jesus Christ for the remission of sins, and ye shall receive the gift of the Holy Ghost." The more we repent, the more evident the Holy Spirit becomes in our lives. He'll replace what repentance has driven out. When an unclean spirit is cast out of a man, it comes back and brings seven more spirits with him. The evicted spirit plus seven others (total eight) is symbolic of a new beginning even in the demonic realm. When we repent we receive forgiveness for our sins but we also receive the gift of the Holy Spirit. He will move into our hearts to occupy the space that was once filled with sin.

> *The presence of the Holy Spirit is another expected bonus of repentance. He loves to hear us repent because it gives Him access and authority to work in various areas of our lives.*

The presence of the Holy Spirit is another expected bonus of repentance. The Holy Spirit loves to hear us repent because it gives Him more access and authority to work in various areas of our lives. David defeated the stronghold of Zion, but then he went to get the Ark of the Covenant. The Bible says that once he went and got the Ark of the

Covenant, he went on and grew great. Repentance helps us reach greatness.

Repentance enables us to take our lives to a higher dimension. We are all capable of reaching higher dimensions through Christ. People always ask what they can do to get to the next dimension. The answer is repent. Repentance gets us ready to live the abundant life God promises His believers. The more serious you treat repentance determines the height of the dimension to which you will advance in God. The Bible talks about this in Psalm 42. It says, "Deep calleth unto deep." Isn't it rewarding to know the more we humble ourselves through repentance and fasting, the higher we can go? Height deals with becoming elevated, and when we become elevated we establish more order in our lives.

> *Repentance is ultimately designed to reveal the heart of God to us.*

Think about the city where you live. Whenever you are stuck in traffic or shopping in a crowded store, things can seem a little chaotic. If you were to board a plane and fly overhead that same city, none of that chaos would be visible because you are viewing it from a different perspective. This is what repentance does; it takes us higher in God and reveals things that "eyes have not seen and ears have not heard" as it is described in the Bible (1 Corinthians 2:9).

Repentance is ultimately designed to reveal the heart of God to us. Once God cleanses our hearts, He can open His

## Chapter Two - The Privilege of Repentance

heart up to us. The Bible says that David was "a man after God's own heart." If you study David's story, you will see that he committed more sins than Saul did. God still chose to use both men despite their faults. An in-depth study reveals that both David and Saul dealt with sin differently. Saul blamed other people for the sins he committed. Whereas once David's sins were revealed to him, he accepted full responsibility and repented. Could it be that the difference between Saul's ministry and David's ministry was their approach to the concept of repentance?

Sometimes people have a hard time applying the principles and lessons we read about in the Bible to their own lives. Repentance is a way for us all to take full responsibility of our own actions. In our homes, schools, government, and even in our churches, we find believers who operate in "The Blame Game," because no one wants to be held accountable. I will be the first person to admit that sometimes things happen to us that are beyond our control, but that does not give us an excuse to allow circumstances to control us. Many people hold onto anger and hurt feelings based on something that happened in the past. Meanwhile, the person responsible for the hurt is oblivious to your pain and insecurity. I am not suggesting you ignore what happened. Accept it, but don't allow yourself to be shackled by it. Be free.

Repentance purges our hearts of any pollutants such as anger, betrayal, resentment, hatred, jealousy, etc. It releases us from past pains whether someone mistreated, misused or abused us. In some cases, we may have been the ones responsible for mistreating, misusing or abusing others. Today is the day to forgive and ask for repentance. If we do not, the enemy will play tricks with our mind, causing us to focus on those negative feelings, thoughts, and behaviors until they consume our very being.

Another privilege of repentance is that it puts a hedge around us. Remember how God put a hedge of protection around Job before He gave the devil permission to destroy all of his possessions? The devil took it one step further and killed his children too. The devil requested for God to also remove the hedge around Job's body, but even then his life was spared. Whenever God allows the hedge to be seasonally lifted, you must know that it is for a divine purpose greater than what we can humanly understand. Job stayed in a penitent posture. He continued to repent while in a state of affliction. Because of his posture of repentance, God renewed the hedge and blessed him with double for his trouble.

CHAPTER THREE

# *The Power of Repentance*

It is important to acknowledge that we can obtain power from repentance. As I have already explained, repentance is not simply a feeling of sorrow or regret related to a previous action, thought or behavior. It is a change or turning away from sinful thoughts or certain morally questionable behavior patterns. Based upon the ministry of John the Baptist, we learn that repentance means to prepare and make ready. John was the forerunner to Jesus. So when we operate in the ministry of John, repentance gets us ready for the ministry of Jesus which is the ministry of salvation and the ministry of ministering to other people. We can never walk into the things of Jesus Christ without first experiencing the ministry of John the Baptist.

John's birth was God's perfect will. God is a God of *Kairos,* which translates to mean divine time. When we study the Word, we see John was born three months before Jesus.

He was on the scene first and then Jesus came. God ordained it this way. Even though He was planning something in the spirit realm, it also had to invade the natural realm. Before we could accept who Jesus was and the purpose for which He was created, God had to first give us instruction on how to accept Him into our hearts. This was done through introducing the ministry of John the Baptist, which represents the ministry of repentance.

Again, repentance is actually a turning over of the heart. The prophet Hosea prophesies the power of repentance. As I mentioned previously, in Hosea chapter 10, he talks about breaking up the fallow ground of your heart because your heart desires to reign down righteousness. The only way we can obtain righteousness is through Jesus Christ because He was perfect and knew no sin. Through Him we can experience the righteousness of God.

Breaking up the fallow ground is a concept that also applies in the natural realm. For example, before a farmer can sow seed they have to till the ground. They take a plow and break up the ground loosening the soil. Afterwards, the ground will be soft enough for the farmer to sow the seed. This is what repentance does – it softens the hearts of hard-hearted people. It turns our hearts over so that we might not only receive the ministry of Jesus Christ but also the Word which is the seed.

Here is the significance: if you look at the ministry of John the Baptist, it gets us ready for the ministry of Jesus Christ

## Chapter Three - The Power of Repentance

which is also representative of the Word, and Jesus, the proverbial seed. Only after the Word is accepted or the seed is planted can the harvest come. Therefore, repentance ultimately sets us up for a harvest. This truth is hidden from us until we understand the power of repentance.

It is common to deny the importance of repentance because it makes us feel dirty. Perhaps you feel like you have fallen short of the glory of God, and in most cases we have. Why should ignorance stop us from taking advantage of another chance to make things right? Sometimes we have to repent not only for the wrong we have done but also the wrongs we have inherited. Sin can attach itself to you based upon the actions of your parents or elements in your environment. In other situations, our sin becomes a habitual cycle and we need to repent over the practice of those habits developed over time.

{ *It is a normal response to feel humbled by the process of repentance. Your own insecurities may be brought to the forefront.* }

My prayer is for God to show me what is hidden in my heart. It is through Him that I have learned to embrace the new perspective of repentance. I now understand that repentance is not a dirty word, although this was not always the case. Before I gained knowledge of the new perspective of repentance, a sense of self-righteousness would creep in and I would make excuses to justify my actions. I want to let you know it is a normal response to feel humbled by the process of repentance. Know that your own insecurities may be brought to the forefront. Just remember, when we repent it serves a larger purpose – we are making our hearts ready. We are preparing for Christ's second coming.

It is wise not to abuse the favor granted to us through repentance. God forbids that we should make conscientious decisions to practice sin. His promise of grace and mercy is not given to us to abuse. We should never abuse God's unconditional love that He has made available to us. By exposing the issues in my heart, I am actually making those areas ready for Jesus Christ.

After we break up the fallow ground of our hearts, as mentioned in Hosea 10, Christ comes in to dwell. The Word which is also known as the [incorruptible] seed gets planted, and the next thing that comes is the harvest. You will not yield a harvest if you refuse to repent. Your enemy's objective is to get you to never repent. When you repent you negate his plan.

From a literal sense, some trees produce fruit, and every fruit has seeds inside. Consider yourself to be a tree. When we possess the spiritual fruit of God, whether love, joy, peace, longsuffering, etc. it will have seed in it. That is why John the Baptist said, "Bring forth fruit to match your repentance." I will not stop repenting until I see the harvest, until I see my behavior change. I should not stop repenting of debt until I see myself no longer in debt and I see the

## Chapter Three - The Power of Repentance

financial abundance. I will not stop repenting until my mouth, movement, and mind line up with the perfect will of God and what the Word demands of His people. I encourage you to do the same. What area of your life do you constantly struggle in? Challenge yourself to think, pray and act according to God's will for your own life.

Philippians 3:12-14 reads, "Not as though I had already attained, either were already perfect: but I follow after, if that I may apprehend that for which also I am apprehended of Christ Jesus. Brethren, I count not myself to have apprehended: but this one thing I do, forgetting those things which are behind, and reaching forth unto those things which are before. "I press toward the mark for the prize of the high calling of God in Christ Jesus."

> *It is wise not to abuse the favor granted to us through repentance. God forbids that we should make conscientious decisions to practice sin. His promise of grace and mercy is not given to us to abuse.*

CHAPTER FOUR

# The Purpose of Repentance

We've talked about the privilege and the power of repentance, but now let's look at the *purpose* of repentance. The New Testament is translated into Greek, even though Jesus spoke Hebrew. The Greek translation of the word *sin* means *to miss the mark*, but it is much more than that. When we sin we are missing more than a mark. We are missing the Kingdom. Ultimately, we are missing our shot to earn eternal life in Heaven. We're missing the more abundant life that God wants us to walk in. The Bible says, "Shall we continue in sin, that grace may abound?" Many of us have the mindset that it is okay to sin. We think that God will look the other way while we do whatever we want and once we finish, God will just forgive us. If we honestly knew what our forgiveness cost, we would not continue to make haphazard decisions. The thoughts we have and the things we do can set us up to fall right into the hands of the enemy. Remember, the enemy wants us to sin.

It gives Satan an opportunity to invoke overwhelming guilt and condemnation into our spirits. Afterward, we begin to feel unworthy of forgiveness, and that is exactly where the enemy wants us. Condemnation makes us not want to repent.

When it comes to repentance, whether we're seeking forgiveness for sin done publically or privately, a lifestyle change is necessary. The enemy dwells in darkness. God is light. To bear sin in our hearts, not repent, and refuse to turn away from those things means we are living in darkness. In essence, we make ourselves vulnerable to the attacks of the enemy because we are operating in his territory. Darkness is Satan's domain. So it comes down to a matter of light and darkness, right versus wrong. Our first step to becoming victorious over the enemy is through repentance; without it, we will certainly remain in the dark. However, when I repent, I expose myself to the light.

> *When it comes to repentance, whether we're seeking forgiveness for sin done publically or privately, a lifestyle change is necessary.*

Picture yourself in a well-lit room. There is one door and no windows. If someone was standing on the other side of that door, you would never know because the door is blocking your stream of vision. When we repent, we remove that door and open up the entrance way to our hearts.

## Chapter Four - The Purpose of Repentance

Take this same illustration. Now turn off all the lights. This is symbolic of what happens when a person becomes born again. We have already repented for previous sins and opened up the door to our hearts but now we must start dealing with the darkness that is hidden inside.

When I accepted Jesus Christ as my Lord and Savior, I became born again according to the traditional church doctrine. Most of you probably went through a similar experience. Through confessing with our mouths and accepting Jesus as the Son of God, we initiated a journey into the darkness of our hearts. The physical anatomy of a human heart includes different sections known as chambers. We can use this biological theory to understand repentance. The sins we commit and our un-Christlike behavior gets hidden in separate corners of our heart. For instance, financial irresponsibility can be stored in one chamber whereas sexual sin may be in another. Whatever your personal issues are, rest assured they will fill our heart until there is no room left. This is why we have to take an active approach to address and resolve them. It is one thing to get saved and open up the door of our hearts, but we also need to repent for the darkness that was already in existence. As a pastor, I often get asked some really tough questions. For example, on more than one occasion people have come to me and inquired about whether it is possible for Christians or Believers to be possessed by demons. The answer is simple. Yes. An individual can believe in God and still be possessed by demons if he or she has never gotten rid of the ones they had before.

The enemy can also gain control of a spiritually born-again believer who has been delivered. The Bible says that when an unclean spirit is cast out of a man, if that man dwells in the enemy's territory he gives evil spirits the right to gain entrance in his life. Sometimes people don't deal with their issues once they get saved, but those things don't just go away on their own! The truth of the matter is we all need to be delivered of unclean spirits and loosed from persistent strongholds. Repentance delivers us from besetting sins. A besetting sin constantly harasses you; it is persistently troublesome. In other words, a besetting sin is the behavioral trap that you keep falling into.

> *Repentance delivers us from besetting sins. A besetting sin is the behavioral trap that you keep falling into.*

In John Chapter 1, the first Scripture reads, "In the beginning was the Word, and the Word was with God and the Word was God. The same was in the beginning with God. All things were made by him; and without him was not anything made that was made. In him was life; and the life was the light of men. And the light shineth in darkness; and the darkness comprehended it not." Notice how the text contrasts light and darkness, specifically in verse 5 which reads, "The light shines in darkness and darkness did not

## Chapter Four - The Purpose of Repentance

comprehend it." The one thing that darkness cannot comprehend is the Word. The Word is life, but the Word is also light, so where the Word is, darkness has to leave.

Now let's refer back to the previous analogy. Imagine yourself in the room with no windows and one door. Immediately after you flip off the light switch, you cannot see anything aside from darkness. But your inability to see does not affect your hearing. Oftentimes, we have to rely on our ability to hear the word of God as guidance out of darkness or, more fittingly, sin. However, if you sit in a dark room long enough, your eyes will adjust making it possible to see what you could not at first. This is precisely the problem for a lot of us - we have adjusted to living in darkness. We can get so comfortable living in the familiar that we begin to develop an ability to see in the dark. If you stay in darkness long enough, when the light finally does come back on, it will take a moment before your eyes readjust to what is normal, or in this case what is godly.

When you study war, military officials often use specific tactics of interrogating prisoners. One common method of intimidation is to put prisoners into a dark room. Military personnel will often punish prisoners by robbing them of all sources of light. This is what the enemy wants to do to us. He wants God's people to dwell in darkness. It is amazing how many of us have adjusted to living in darkness.

Notice in John 1:5, the Bible refers to light and life which is what God and His Word represents. The imagery of darkness refers to Satan. In verse 6, the Scripture shifts gears. It reads, "There was a man sent from God, whose name was John." First, the text talks about light and darkness, then switches to the subject of John and how he would bear witness of the Light. Without doing an in-depth study, the revelation here may be easily overlooked. The Bible says, "It is the glory of God to conceal a thing, but it is the honor of a king to search a matter out."

John's name is translated to mean grace. When we are introduced to John, look what happens in verse 7. "The same came for a witness, to bear witness of the Light, that all men through him might believe." John came to be a witness but he wasn't the Light. The revelation here involves the significance of repentance. John's mother was Elizabeth; his father was Zacharias. John was born three months before Jesus, Our Savior. It could be no other way because John's ministry prepares us for a clearer understanding of why Jesus was sent to the earth.

When we start taking the matter of repentance seriously, it allows us to take one step toward ensuring our eternity in Heaven.

All four synoptic gospels, Matthew, Mark, Luke and John talk about John the Baptist. Let's take a look at Luke chapter 3:2-4, "Annas and Caiaphas being the high priests, the word of God came unto John the son of Zacharias in the wilderness. And he came into all the country about Jordan, preaching the baptism of repentance for the remission of

## Chapter Four - The Purpose of Repentance

sins; As it is written in the book of the words of Esaias the prophet saying, "The voice of one crying in the wilderness, Prepare ye the way of the Lord make his paths straight."

In Mark 1:1-4, "The beginning of the gospel of Jesus Christ, the Son of God; As it is written in the prophets, Behold I send my messenger before thy face, which shall prepare the way before thee. The voice of one crying in the wilderness, Prepare ye the way of the Lord, make his paths straight. John did baptize in the wilderness, and preach the baptism of repentance for the remission of sins."

Matthew 3:1-3 reads, "In those days came John the Baptist, preaching in the wilderness of Judea, And saying, Repent ye: for the kingdom of heaven is at hand. For this is he that was spoke of by the prophet Esaias, saying, The voice of one crying in the wilderness, prepare ye the way of the Lord, make his paths straight."

The common denominator in each of these Scripture verses is that John was in the wilderness. He was preaching the baptism of repentance. John was the voice of "the one crying in the wilderness" saying, "Prepare and make ready the way of the Lord." The ministry of John or repentance gets us ready for the next step - inviting and accepting Christ into our hearts. When I repent, I am walking in the ministry of John the Baptist. John said, "I must decrease that He might increase."

Repentance gets us ready for a number of things. First and foremost, repentance gets us ready for the increase of

Jesus as He arrives on the scene. When we repent, Christ can come into our hearts. The devil tries to distract us with guilt and condemnation by exposing our sin. In reality though, this works in our favor because it causes us to direct our attention on a need for change. Every time you repent, your heart becomes more prepared. The word *prepare* means *to make ready beforehand.* Your heart becomes more prepared to become the "manger of Christ." Every believer knows Jesus was born in a manger because there was no room for Him in the inn. Today Jesus passes by so many of us because our hearts are overcrowded with too much stuff. He will appeal to the prostitute who is willing to repent or the drug dealer who is crying out for God's presence. He will also attract that molested child whose situation has brought them to a place of brokenness and desperation. These people are reaching out to God and making room for Him in their hearts, whereas sometimes saints sit in church and act like we don't have any issues. We have our outer appearances together, but are not dealing with the mess in our chests.

Repentance is a personal experience. I can repent for others and their wrongdoings, but no one can repent for my sin like I can. I know what's in my heart just like you know what's in yours. Don't despise repentance. Every time God shows us something we need to repent for we should give Him praise. When was the last time you praised the Lord for the spirit of repentance hitting your life? The reason some of

## Chapter Four - The Purpose of Repentance

us do not value repentance is because we lack knowledge. Every season of significant spiritual growth and maturity in your walk with God will be prefaced by a time of deep repentance. So before God gives you more Jesus, you have to do more with John.

John the Baptist told the people that someone would be coming after him whose shoe laces he was unworthy of tying. He did not feel worthy enough to be in the same vicinity with Jesus, but John was privileged to baptize Jesus. I imagine John probably felt like Jesus should have been baptizing him instead. However, we know God does things in decency and in order. Since Jesus accepted the ministry of John and submitted to it, why don't you? We all have issues in our hearts. We can spend all of our time and money fixing everything on the outside, but the internal problems will still remain until we get a true revelation of repentance. Once we finally get it, our lifestyle will change.

John's ministry of repentance does not merely make a man or woman apologetic, it makes them ready. When we repent and ask God to forgive us of specific sins, we are saying more than "I'm sorry." We are making a confession that we are ready to experience more of Jesus in our lives. Then God knows we are ready to receive Christ, the Strengthener, the Anointed One, and His anointing.

I want Jesus Christ for who He is and all He represents. If you have never accepted your rightful gift of salvation, you need Jesus to save you. Before He can do that, He has to strengthen you. Repentance is the first step. John the Baptist said 'prepare ye the way, make his path straight." The more I repent and turn away from sin in various areas of my life, the more I get rid of crookedness and my paths become straighter. The Bible says 'straight and narrow is the way that leads to eternal life.'

Repentance is God's way of perfecting us. Without it, we can never achieve true perfection. Look at the Church of Laodicea in Revelations 3:19-20, "As many as I love, I rebuke and chasten: be zealous therefore, and repent. Behold, I stand at the door and knock: if any man hear my voice, and open the door, I will come in to him and will sup with him, and he with me." God tells us to be eager when it comes to repentance. It is a vital aspect in the overall sphere of spiritual maturity. Absolute repentance means to turn over the soil of our hearts for a new planting of kingdom concepts, kingdom direction, and kingdom revelation.

> *Absolute repentance means to turn over the soil of our hearts for a new planting of kingdom concepts, kingdom direction, and kingdom revelation.*

Remember, God said repent for "the kingdom is at hand." He never said anything about repenting because the church is at hand. Repentance gets us ready for something bigger and better than the church; it gets us ready for the kingdom. And what we need is for the kingdom to come so that God's will can be

## Chapter Four - The Purpose of Repentance

done. Jesus said it is the father's good pleasure to give us the kingdom, but we will never tap into the kingdom without repentance. Some people are not willing to repent because they are not really willing to let go of whatever they are on repenting for. The moment they let go and take repentance seriously, they will have no problem lying prostrate before the Lord.

When people repented in the Old Testament, they wore sackcloth and mourned. It was an outward sign of spiritual death. In other words they were dying to themselves and their own selfish desires. Many people are so busy judging everyone else they do not take time to focus on themselves and their own inefficiencies. Are you one of those people? Are you dealing with the stuff in your heart?

John the Baptist had a unique purpose; he was expected to immerse the entire nation of Israel into an attitude of repentance. He was sent by God before the coming of Christ and given the task to prepare and make ready the way of the Lord. God wants to establish an attitude of repentance in us so we will consistently return to Him. The result is the fruit of righteousness flourishing in our lives. We should never stop repenting until our sin is replaced with the character and the attributes of Christ. For example, a thief should never stop repenting until they do not practice stealing anymore and they become people who can give freely without hidden agendas. Another prime example is someone who is hateful. They should continue to repent for their hateful attitude until they understand the true meaning of love and walk freely in it.

Repentance is powerful but repentance is not easy. We need divine enablement. We need the Holy Ghost to help us accomplish this spiritual principle, much like we need help dealing with forgiveness. A whole lot of people find it hard to forgive others because they are trying to do it in their own strength. Zechariah said it's "not by power, nor by might, but by His Spirit" (Zechariah 4:6). Thus, repentance is a spiritual principle. It is a divine kingdom word. The devil does not like it when you apply kingdom principles to your life. He hates it when you go to God and repent. He becomes infuriated when you seriously repent because he has to relinquish his hold on that area of your life.

Repentance marks the beginning of our spiritual deliverance. Asking for God's forgiveness and repenting before Him, are like a sweet smelling cologne or perfume that draws God closer to us. Our repentance is a pleasant aroma to Him and it travels directly from our hearts to His.

Repentance is a spiritual repellant. It repels the devil and his demons much like the insect repellant Off! that gets rid of insects and mosquitoes. God tells us to repent for the remission of our sins. In the book of Leviticus, we learn that there cannot be any remission of sins without the shedding of blood. Jesus, being the perfect sacrifice, has taken care of that "shedding of blood" part so that we don't have to continuously kill bullocks and lambs. He was that perfect

## Chapter Four - The Purpose of Repentance

lamb that shed His own blood on Calvary's cross so that the sin of the world can be taken away. So whoever believes upon Him can have their sins remitted by God. When we seek repentance, we are also making a request to the Lord. We are saying, "Lord, I want you to wash me in the blood." Wherever there is the acceptance of His blood, Christ can come and abide. Again, this is why Pentecost followed Passover.

Sadly enough, believers often miss the revelation of John. There are far too many arrogant, proud saints who think too highly of themselves. God is not looking for great men. Instead, He's looking for humble people through whom He can do great things. For Jesus says, "Greater works can you do because I go to my Father" (John 14:12). He wants to do great things through us by His Spirit. It is our responsibility to make sure we are in a place where God can use us greatly.

Our spiritual walk is a personal thing. You should not focus on what other people are doing. The more you deal with the "log in your eye" through repentance, the more compassionate you will be about dealing with a little straw in your brother's eye. The concept works both ways. Sometimes we have the straw and somebody else may have the log. Either way, you definitely want to deal with your own faults before trying to address the faults in others.

> *Repentance prepares the heart for righteousness. It unlocks the power of our faith in God.*

Repentance prepares the heart for righteousness. It unlocks the power of our faith in God. If you refuse to repent and are unwilling to accept the ministry of John the Baptist, you are admitting that you do not want to change. Change is an essential part of repentance. Sometimes the mere thought of repentance and change can make us feel and sense of unworthiness. It may make you feel like God is angry or upset with you. However, God's anger is not the reason why He requires repentance. The opposite is true; it's His lovingkindness. The Bible clearly states that it is the goodness of the Lord that leads us to repentance (Romans 2:4).

> *The strong conviction of repentance is God pulling us to come to Him. He's telling us to "make ready" as a reassurance of His great love toward us.*

Whenever you get a revelation to repent, it is not the devil. The strong conviction of repentance is God pulling us to come to Him. He's telling us to make ready as reassurance of His great love toward us. Sadly, we can continue to walk around with pride and hardened hearts ignoring those tugs. We allow ourselves to be burdened down because we refuse to repent due to a desire to avoid change. Only repentance causes demonic spirits and negative experiences to leave our lives. Once those things are released, you have to relinquish them. What happens too often on the contrary is that we do not want to relinquish or abandon those feelings, behavioral patterns or

## Chapter Four - The Purpose of Repentance

lifestyles. Instead, we maintain them based upon the pleasures they give us. At times those pleasures can seem overwhelmingly attractive to us, more so than the presence of Christ, causing us to cling to them with a tight grip in our hearts. This is why it takes the divine enablement of God's goodness and lovingkindness to break the strong grip we have on sinful pleasures.

I just mentioned that God's goodness leads us to repentance. In addition, Jeremiah 31:3 reveals that God's lovingkindness will draw us to Him. So, we must realize that repentance is so much more than a heartfelt apology. We have to see it as God calling us to Him. By this, we must make a personal acclamation that we are ready and we have a desire to get prepared and walk on the straight and narrow path. This is us acknowledging that the ministry of John precedes the ministry of Jesus. One could not exist without the other.

> *We must realize that repentance is so much more than a heartfelt apology. We have to see it as God calling us to Him.*

Even Isaiah knew this. In addition to saying, "Lo a virgin will be with child" (Isaiah 7:14), he also said there will be a voice of "One crying in the wilderness, prepare ye the way and make the path straight'" (Isaiah 40:3). Isaiah prophesied about Jesus, but he also prophesied about John the Baptist who would later warn the Pharisees and Sadducees about the wrath to come. He told them that the axe was laid at the tree and they should bring forth the fruit to match their repentance (Matthew 3:7-8). However, the religious Pharisees did not repent. It is difficult to convince a hypocrite to repent because they are too busy trying to look pious for people. They failed to realize that God looks at the heart, not the outward appearance. If only our hearts were as clean as our church suits, then we would be on our way to kingdom living! It's time to come clean!

Repentance represents a spiritual cleansing and is illustrated throughout the Bible with the typology of physical cleanliness. Again, one great example of this is in the book of Malachi where he refers to the *fuller's soap*. The fuller's soap is a substance that shepherds used centuries ago. Fuller's soap had a good lather and was strong enough to get beneath sheep's wool and clean away any infections. It would also kill the insects that would burrow underneath the thick wool. A similar process happens when we repent. There are so many sins that burrow down in our hearts and the word of God is like fuller's soap which lathers and soaks into the crevices of our hearts to loosen up and wash away the impurities rooted deeply within.

Once we've bathed ourselves in the cleansing power of Jesus' blood and His Word, we can seek the Holy Ghost's presence and His anointing. The book of Proverbs talks about an apothecary. This is someone who makes drugs or medicines. He also specialized in preparing different ointments, fragrances and oils. The Scripture says that when a fly gets into a perfume bottle, it drowns and ruins the perfume. How is this theory applicable to repentance? Think about it; if you put on perfume without taking a bath first, you will still stink. We must accept John the Baptist's teachings in order to usher in the return of Jesus Christ. If we're going to experience the power of repentance we've got to accept the ministry of John the Baptist. The more we repent, the more we make ourselves ready, the more we come clean; we will begin to experience the authentic, life changing power of God. And we should never stop until we are perfected in Christ.

CHAPTER FIVE

# The Process of Repentance

The New American Standard Bible says we shall be saved through repentance and rest (Isaiah 30:15). In my opinion, this is another reference to John and Jesus. Jesus represents rest, while John represents repentance or *returning*. Statistics show that the word *return* appears in the Bible 263 times. The word *repent* appears 46 times. In the Old Testament when God said, "*Return* to me," what He was really saying was "Repent." The two terms are synonymous.

In Isaiah 30:15 God says, "In repentance and rest you will be saved, in quietness and trust is your strength, but you were not willing." The issue was that the Children of Israel refused to repent. God offers them unshakable confidence but the people simply would not part from their rebellious behavior. The greatest revelation in this Scripture is the relationship between repentance and rest. We must realize that we can't have *rest* unless we *repent*.

## Coming Clean

There is an obvious difference between saying, "I'm sorry," and true repentance. Peter and Judas are good examples. These two disciples teach us a valuable lesson – who we repent to matters. The Bible tells us Jesus specifically chose His disciples. We know that Judas betrayed Jesus with a holy kiss and for 30 pieces of silver. Although it was prophetic that Judas would betray Him, he still had an opportunity to make things right. When he felt bad about what he did, he went to the people and tried to return the money but it was not enough to free Judas from the guilt. He was sorry but he went to the wrong people to express his remorse. He didn't go to God. We later learn that Judas' guilt drove him to hang himself. However, his life did not have to end so drastically. Judas' *betrayal* was not much worse than Peter's *denial* of Jesus. The difference is seen in how they responded. Judas repented to the scribes, the Pharisees, the Kings and government officials. The main point is Judas failed to repent to the proper person and this caused him to miss his call to Biblical repentance.

In comparison, let's look at Peter who denied Jesus three times. When Jesus prophesied it would happen (not once, but three times), Peter refused to accept it. Luke 22:60 reads, "And Peter said, Man, I know not what thou sayest.

> *Judas' betrayal was not much worse than Peter's denial of Jesus. The difference is seen in how they responded.*

## Chapter Five - The Process of Repentance

And immediately, while he yet spake, the cock crew. And the Lord turned, and looked upon Peter. And Peter remembered the word of the Lord, how he had said unto him, before the cock crow, thou shalt deny me thrice. And Peter went out, and wept bitterly." The Amplified Bible says, "He [Peter] went out and wept bitterly", that is with painful, moving grief. Peter denies Jesus three times but went to God and repented. Judas, on the other hand, betrayed Jesus and afterwards went to the people to apologize.

Remember the first day of the week when the sisters went to the tomb and Jesus wasn't there? Who did they go tell that Jesus was no longer in that borrowed tomb? You got it – Peter and John. When the disciples realized what had happened, Peter and John went running toward the tomb. John gets there first but he does not go inside. When Peter gets there, he steps inside the tomb. He looks at the place where Jesus' body had laid and finds the linen (grave clothes) folded neatly like a napkin.

I have to interject something here about the Jewish culture. It is customary tradition to eat Matzah bread. During the Passover holiday, the Jews would take the Matzah bread, divide it, serve one half, and store the rest. Occasionally the father would use the Matzah bread to play a game with the children. This is discussed in more detail in chapter seven about Peter's take on Repentance.

One of the first steps toward repentance is admitting your wrong. This is exemplified in the story of the prodigal son as told in Luke 15. Most of you are probably familiar with what happens. A father has two sons between whom he divided his estate. The youngest one gathered all he had, left home and went to a country far away. He spent all he had and then a famine came. This son had lost his wealth and now he had to get a job feeding pigs just to make enough money to buy food to eat. Then in verse 17, it says "And when he came to himself, he said, 'How many hired servants of my father's have bread enough and to spare, and I perish with hunger!'" The Bible tells us that the Prodigal son realized his faults, returned to his father and asked for forgiveness. He was even prepared to put in work and effort to regain his father's trust. However, when his father saw him coming from a distance, he was so happy to see him again that he prepared a celebration in his honor. The father welcomed his son with open arms.

The story of the prodigal son teaches us that true biblical repentance is a combination of three things:

1. Repentance includes conviction. In conviction, you feel what God feels about your sin. Conviction includes both your emotions and expressions. Your heart is affected, not just your words.
2. Repentance includes confession. In confession, you agree with God that you have sinned. Confession includes both your mind and mouth.
3. Repentance includes change. In change, you stop

## Chapter Five - The Process of Repentance

worshipping sin and start worshipping Jesus. Change includes your attitude and actions.

The prodigal son models this true repentance; he has a change of heart and felt convicted about the sins he committed against both his Heavenly and earthly fathers. He then confessed his unworthiness and committed in his heart to change by asking to be treated as one of his father's hired servants. Once we do these three things, true biblical repentance can take place. Just as the father celebrated his son's return, God does the same thing for us. When He sees us ready to come clean and answer the call to repentance, He will throw a party welcoming us back home. It gives the Father great joy to see us repent from our sins and turn away from the very things that separated us from Him in the first place.

When Jesus died on the cross for our sins, He did it to become our Savior. At a certain point in our life, someone came and witnessed Christ to us and we felt the spirit of conviction. Then we repented and came to know Jesus Christ as our personal Savior. John lo:27-29 says, "My sheep hear my voice, and I know them, and they follow me: and I give unto them eternal life; and they shall never perish, neither shall any man pluck them out of my hand, My Father, which gave them me, is greater than all; and no man is able to pluck them out of my Father's hand." Notice however, the Scripture never said that we could not walk out of God's presence like the prodigal son left the presence of his earthly father.

In this story our attention is drawn to the one who left home. If you look at the text in Luke 15 again, there are two brothers. One might assume that the son who remained at home would have developed a strong relationship with his father. Even though he was closer in physical proximity than his brother, this particular son was still out of fellowship with the father. The concept of repentance can also apply to believers who are in the physical House of God but are backslidden in their spiritual walk with Christ. And it happens more often than we realize. You can be a pulpit preacher, choir member, or fill the role of a musician, usher or church staff member and become backslidden. You can be physically present in the church while your heart can be far from God. Be careful where your heart is, because your body will eventually follow. It is not uncommon for an individual to leave a place because their heart is somewhere else.

Just like the tugging on our heart towards repentance begins inwardly, that pull to backslide begins inside of us too. People actually allow their heart to leave God first before

## Chapter Five - The Process of Repentance

they physically leave the church. Just because we're in church lifting up our hands does not mean we're in relationship with God. In Matthew 15, Jesus quotes the prophet Esaias, when he said, "This people draweth nigh unto me with their mouth and honoreth me with their lips; but their heart is far from me."

1 Corinthians 1:9 says, "God is faithful, by whom ye were called unto the fellowship of his Son Jesus Christ our Lord." The word *fellowship* here is synonymous with *relationship*. When God created Adam, He wanted a relationship with Mankind. Yet God kicked Adam and Eve out of the Garden of Eden as a repercussion of their disobedience. Why did He respond that way? Because Adam and Eve allowed themselves to be deceived, forfeited their relationship with God, and ultimately became disconnected from Him.

In the book of Luke, the Bible tells us that the prodigal son took his journey into a far country and wasted his substance with riotous living. However, nowhere in the Scripture is it ever mentioned that the father left home to find his son. Instead, the son returned back to the father. One might wonder why he even left home in the first place. What made the prodigal son depart from his fellowship with his father? He wanted to fulfill a sense of entitlement; he desired material possessions and worldly affluence.

This is particularly interesting because when Jesus came to Earth and died for us, He became a Savior. His mission was to come, seek and save those who were lost (Luke

19:10). Jesus came after us. The approach seems to become more indirect for a believer who has accepted salvation yet finds himself backsliding. God tends to become more passive aggressive; He does not continue to send Jesus Christ – His work is completed until the Second Coming. On the contrary, I believe God uses circumstances and situations to get our attention so that we, just like the prodigal son, can come running back to Him.

All too often Christians start their spiritual journey on fire for God. We'd do whatever He wanted us to do. We would read our Bible every day, witness to others and religiously showed up for church services. When I first fell in love with God, I was the same way. I stayed up all night reading my Word and I would witness to everyone. God didn't have to beg me to go to church. As a matter of fact, I found church services to attend. Why? Because I had a new fellowship and I wanted to nurture that relationship with a sense of urgency. I attended Sunday school and then went to the church service that followed. Afterwards, I would go home and read the Word all night. When I worked as a car salesman, I'd answer the phone, "Praise the Lord, this is Anthony Knotts." On my break, I would read my Bible. I was on fire for God. I was a Christian; I was going to heaven and I didn't care who knew it. But what happens?

We can get to a place and position where God starts to prosper us. He starts blessing us; situations and circumstances start working out better for us. Then just like

## Chapter Five - The Process of Repentance

the prodigal son, we set ourselves up for a downfall. For me, all the things God started to bless me with made me lose sight of Him.

At the time I was called to pastor, I started holding church services in my apartment. Membership started to grow and God eventually blessed me with two buildings. I had nice cars and began to develop influence in the community which paved the way for me to travel across the nation and overseas. I met lots of people and started hanging out with some pastors of big megachurches. It's amazing how you can lose yourself in the glitz and glam. While we're doing all these activities, our longing for God goes unnoticed, unaddressed, and unfulfilled. Those nights where you'd be studying your Word for hours and those times when you'd wake up at 5AM every morning to seek His face just because you were so thirsty for God are no longer a concern. Your focus shifted to something of lesser importance. In my case, I became too concerned and distracted with buildings and budgets and upholding my public image.

If we're completely honest, some of us will admit that our prayer life is suffering or our habit of fasting seems more difficult to do now than it used to. If you're not careful, those days of selflessly seeking God will be far behind you. Like Samson, you'll wake up and shake yourself not realizing that Delilah has cut the locks of your hair because she's found where your strength lies. The ironic thing is that Samson still felt the presence of God because He hadn't totally lifted. You can go around people and still quote the Word. You know how to be a Christian by looking the part. Unfortunately, the institution of church has taught believers how to 'fake' our spiritual walk with God. However, for those who truly know Him, you cannot ignore that still, small voice in your heart that asks, "When are you going to spend some time with me?" Red flags may start going off when you compare your current behavior to what you used to do when your relationship with God was green. For someone who may be reading this book, your relationship with God may be suffering, while at the same time your relationships with people are growing. So now you may be too busy to meet with God because you're in demand. Everybody wants to get with you and consume your time. My friend, your popularity may be at the expense of you losing yourself and the intimacy you've developed with the Father. I wrote this book for you to come clean and restore a right relationship with your Father. He's waiting with open arms to celebrate your return.

*The life changing story that Jesus told of the prodigal son should teach us how to be cautious of the pursuit of stuff. Seeking material things can make us lose sight of who we really are. It can also make us walk out on the most important relationship - our relationship with the Father.*

The life changing story that Jesus told of the prodigal son should teach us how to be cautious of the pursuit of stuff.

## Chapter Five - The Process of Repentance

Seeking material things can make us lose sight of who we really are. It can also make us walk out on the most important relationship - our relationship with the Father. I praise God because everything I lost, God knew I could afford to lose it. He allowed things to go wrong in my life just to teach me a lesson. I believe the father in this story is like God – he represents wisdom. God is wise enough to know the outcome that we need and it far exceeds the existence of material possessions or social status.

Referring back to the Scriptures in Luke 15, there is not much detail about what happens once the prodigal son reached his destination. I believe he attracted relationships with the wrong people. This often happens when someone gains wealth and has obtained a certain status in society. A similar occurrence happened to me. Years ago, when I lost myself and my sight of God, I became more compelled to boast my image. Everyone wanted to be a part of my life. I was asked to join legislative boards in the community because of what God made me. However, I failed to realize that I was just walking in the results of those days when I would wake up early in the morning, read the Word of God, and sow a spiritual seed into my heart. When I began to experience these results I ceased from planting sufficient spiritual seeds. If you ever find yourself in a similar situation, a famine will surely come, if it hasn't already.

It is foolish to assume you are capable of a continuous harvest when you stop planting seeds. I use the term sowing as a symbolic reference to getting in God's presence, studying His Word, and panting after God. It would be wise to avoid making the same mistakes I did. Avoid overindulgence in your spiritual harvest without replenishing your seeds because ultimately your relationship with God will suffer. Once I was attracted to the wrong people and drawn away from my pure love of God, I began to experience the flaming fire in my heart for God beginning to flicker out like that one small candle left on a little toddler's birthday cupcake.

What makes us leave fellowship with God? In Luke 15, another parallel can be established between the prodigal son and the born again believer who has lost fellowship with our heavenly Father. The Bible lets us know that it wasn't long before hard circumstances hit the prodigal son's life to get his attention. Soon after he spent all his fortune, he began to be in want. The Bible says that he "came to himself." Then in verse 18, the prodigal son says, "I will arise and go to my father, and will say unto him, Father, I have sinned against heaven and before thee, and am no more worthy to be called thy son: make me as one of thy hired servants."

Sin is dangerous because it causes us to get out of fellowship with God. We often view sin as adultery, homosexuality or other obvious things that are done outside the presence of God. It is, however, just as dangerous to declare your abstinence or avoidance of sin but still remain outside the presence of God. This is called "being religious."

## Chapter Five - The Process of Repentance

For example, the Pharisees were so cautious about what they did, but failed to realize how judgmental they had become. They began to point the finger at people. Jesus talked about them being like dead tombs. The Bible speaks against judging each other. You may not commit the same sin someone else may have committed but it does not make you any better than them. Perhaps you harbor a sinful thought in your mind or did something "un-Christlike" in the privacy of your own home. You must come clean if you hear God calling you to a place of repentance.

To backslide is initially a mental state which later proliferates into an action or behavior. Are you still panting after God the way a deer pants for water? Some people leave Christ and they walk away from church completely. Others will leave Christ but remain among the church body. I prefer to define sin as disobedience of God's will in whatever form. I know talking about sin and backsliding is a touchy subject. Please do not put this book down, give it away, or throw it in the trash. I promise you that if you yield to the process your life will drastically change for the better.

> *Some people leave Christ and they walk away from church completely. Others will leave Christ but remain among the church body.*

Consider Adam and Eve; they did not commit adultery or murder anyone. Instead, they ate fruit from the tree of the knowledge of good and evil, something God told them not to do (Genesis 2:17). They disobeyed God's instructions and when they did so, they sinned against Him. What about Matthew 6:33 where God tells us, "Seek ye first the kingdom of God and His righteousness" or Colossians 3:2 which tells us to "set our affections on the things above"? Are we obeying God's Word? 1 Peter 5:6 tells us, "Humble ourselves under the mighty hand of God and He shall exalt us in due time." What about these Scriptures and others? What about His commands? What about, "Let everything that has breath praise the Lord"? "And it's not in us to know our own ways and direct our steps"? When we fail to obey the things written in God's Word we are being disobedient. These are mere examples of the instructions God has given us to protect our relationship and our fellowship with Him.

Instead of holding ourselves accountable, we look at people and justify our sin by comparing what we do to what others have done. The reality is that if we are not studying to show ourselves approved (2 Timothy 2:15), praying without ceasing (1 Thessalonians 5:23) and other fundamental things, then there's no telling what we might find ourselves doing. Are you doing things that will build your relationship with God? Are you communicating with Him? Do you tell God how much you love Him? Have you forsaken the assembling of the saints? Are you forsaking the opportunity to come boldly before the throne of grace? The consequence of disobedience materializes in two different forms in our lives:

## Chapter Five - The Process of Repentance

(1) You can become a hypocrite or
(2) You can backslide publicly.

The difference is a hypocrite assumes position within the church. Meanwhile, a backslider usually leaves the church, if only for a temporary period of time. The common denominator is a heart that is not in tune with God.

In Luke 10:38-42, we read the story of Jesus visiting Martha's house. Isn't it interesting that Martha had such a disapproving perception of Mary? In contrast, Mary said nothing about Martha. Mary took advantage of the situation and was immediately occupied with sitting in the presence of Jesus; Martha was too distracted and spent most of her time trying to serve Jesus. Mary was at Jesus's feet, while Martha was busy preparing dinner.

It's amazing how distractions can change the condition of our hearts toward God. I was so busy serving people that I ended up leaving my fellowship with Jesus Christ. Being a pastor does not guarantee that you'll be free from backsliding. At one point, I simply became overwhelmed by the burden of meeting the needs of people. Buildings, budgets and payrolls took precedence and caused extreme fatigue. Like many pastors around the globe, I was experiencing a burnout. I'm not a quitter, but there were times when the option was tempting.

We should all aspire to be more like Mary, sitting at Jesus's feet. That's how you maintain that intimate relationship with Him. The sooner we understand the prodigal son and the blessing of "coming to ourselves," which has nothing to do with possessions or position, the better off we will be. When the prodigal son came to himself, he was so desperate to get back into the presence of his father that he was even willing to take a demotion. That's the same attitude we should have.

Do you thirst for God's presence or are you after the presents he can give? If you have a heart for God, you don't have to base your life on material things. He tells us that He'll supply our every need according to His riches in glory (Philippians 4:19). Remember Matthew 6:33 where it instructs us to "Seek ye first the kingdom of God and all of His righteousness"? Well, it further states that when you seek His kingdom that "All these things shall be added unto you." In other words, material needs (and sometimes wants) will be materialized in your life. You don't have to worry about obtaining them; God will make sure that He gets them to you. In Psalm 91, God says that whoever dwells in the Secret Place will have peace, provision and protection. The key is abiding in His presence. We need to stay at the feet of a loving God like Mary did.

For many of us, our spiritual survival is dependent upon an old fellowship with God. But where are you in your personal relationship with Him now? Learn from my mistake - there's only a limited amount of time where you can live off a harvest from seeds you've previously sown. Right now you need to check your heart. Where is it? If you're not careful, you'll find yourself grasping for a relationship with the Father. When you attempt to fill the void by spending more time with a significant other or being occupied with your job or other extracurricular activities, you need to come to yourself like the prodigal son did. You need to have a reality check. You need a Coming Clean moment.

We really have to be careful about the condition of our hearts. This issue is mentioned in Hosea 10:12 when Hosea asked God to break up the fallow ground of his heart and rain down His righteousness. His heart had become hard. In Ezekiel 36:26, He promised to remove our heart of stone and give us a heart of flesh. To have a *heart of flesh* means your heart is sensitive to God. It means you are often convicted of wrongdoing if you step outside of His will.

Contrary to the heart of flesh is the *heart of stone* (stony heart). There are times when our hearts become hard - too hard to yield to spiritual convictions and kingdom obligations. Various situations and experiences can affect your perception. They can have a negative impact on your heart. A hard heart makes it much easier to ignore the voice of God. Sin will also dull your spiritual ears making it difficult to hear God's voice. It'll darken your eyes to the point where you can't see. You can read the Bible but still lack revelation of the Word. Sin will divert your feet; it will have you walking in the opposite direction of God and where He told you to go.

The bible says "the steps of a good man are ordered by the Lord." If you're walking in sin, God cannot order your steps.

Once you realize you have walked away from the presence of God, there is at least one major step to take before you can get back to where you were. Again, let's refer to the story of the prodigal son. When he realized his faults, he came to himself and he repented for what he'd done. Then he returned back home and got back in his father's presence. It is so easy to get distracted with what is in our hearts. The prodigal son placed too much value in his portion of goods and in the end he had nothing left to show for it. The same thing can happen to us. If we are not careful, we will start to think too highly of our gifts and our focus shifts away from the source from which our gifts originated.

True enough, Adam caused the fall of man through his disobedience. However, Jesus Christ was born, bled and died to right Adam's wrongs. Upon accepting salvation, the Bible tells us to confess with our mouths and believe in our hearts that Jesus Christ is Lord and that God raised Him from the dead (Romans 10:9, 10). From that very moment, we are no longer at liberty to blame Adam for our downfalls, failures or sinful nature. If we happen to backslide, it is based upon a conscious decision that we make. If we take our heart away from God and put it somewhere else, it is our choice. God knows our vulnerability and the possibility of us choosing the opposite of His will. This is why He tells us to guard our

## Chapter Five - The Process of Repentance

hearts with all diligence because out of it flows the issues of life (Proverbs 4:23).

God wants our heart and so does the enemy. When you look at 1 Thessalonians, it talks about the son of perdition and how the spirit of the antichrist is looking to rule the throne. In a spiritual sense, the throne represents your heart. Satan will never be able to rule the throne in heaven so now he wants to rule the throne of your heart. He wants to sit right where God is supposed to sit because Satan knows that whoever reigns on your heart will run your life.

In Revelations 2, John writes to the church of Ephesus (one of the seven churches of the Asia Minor). Each church is representative of the state of those churches then, now, and prophetically of the conditions of a believer's personal walk with God today. The Scripture says, "Unto the angel of the church of Ephesus write; these things saith he that holdeth the seven stars in his right hand, who walketh in the midst of seven golden candlesticks; I know thy works, and thy labour and thy patience, and how thou canst not bear them which are evil; and thou hast tried them which say they are apostles, and are not, and hast found them liars: and hast borne, and hast patience, and for my name's sake hast labored, and hast not fainted." This passage points out the church's work, patience, and disgust of evil things.

The members used their spiritual gift of discernment to determine who was truly called by God. For the Lord's sake, they labored without getting tired. They were able to discern false apostles and prophets but couldn't discern their own spiritual depletion. This proves that we can operate in spiritual gifts and yet have hearts not aligned with God. We must be careful because our work can be done in vain. Perhaps, this is why Jesus said in Matthew 7 that God will turn away workers of iniquity. "Many will say to me in that day, Lord, Lord have we not prophesied in thy name? And in thy name have cast out devils? And in thy name done many wonderful works? And then will I profess unto them, I never knew you: depart from me, ye that work iniquity."

Instead of being iniquity workers let's be penitent people of faith. Let's be those passionate believers chasing after God and allowing Him to inhabit our hearts. When we are this way, we can obtain a sincere compassion toward the people of God as well. Jesus is a perfect example. He knew God the Father loved the people so He had compassion for the people that the Father loved. Jesus Christ saw fit to carry out His mission of salvation on the earth because He knew the intense love that the Father had for us. With this in mind, how can we ever say we love God, but lack compassion for His people (or any people)? Jesus, like a great High Priest, was touched by the feelings of our infirmities. He was moved by what we were going through and He was overwhelmed with compassion, insomuch that He did something about it – He died for our sins. This was the highest form of love. It was agape love.

## Chapter Five - The Process of Repentance

I'm quite sure you've heard of the three forms of love – agape, phileo and eros. *Agape* love is a selfless love from one person to another without sexual implications. It is self-sacrificing. Agape love is not selective. You can't just say, "I love God, but I hate that person" or "I'm not going to forgive them." That is not an option. Meanwhile *phileo* love is a fraternal love like one you would have for a sibling. We call this "brotherly" love. It's giving someone else respect and being courteous to them but you don't necessarily have to be compassionate toward them. *Eros*, of course, is more sensual in nature and carries a sexual connotation. When it comes to the love of God, or agape love, we lose the option to pick and choose whom we wish to love. This teaches us humility. If we're going to love people the way Jesus did we've got to humble ourselves and not be picky about whom we're going to serve. Part of coming clean is preparing ourselves to serve whom God instructs us to serve without motive for personal gain. Don't limit yourself to a certain demographic. Be ready to spread the love of God to anyone He puts in your path to serve.

God wants to stretch your ability to love. Sometimes we can walk around not wanting to do the things of God when we should actually see it as a privilege. I know it can be challenging at times. And sometimes God would have us to do things at the most inconvenient time, like times we set aside for ourselves. But God created us and redeemed us to do what He asks of us and to do it when He asks it of us. If we don't see it as a privilege we'll begin to make all kinds of excuses as to why we can't do what He asks. This can ultimately lead us into a backslidden condition or even reprobate. The old saints would say, "Saying 'No' to God is just like saying 'Yes' to Satan."

This is similar to what happened at the church of Ephesus. The members seemed to be diligent at doing good things. They were patient and believed in a righteous way of life. As I stated before, the Church of Ephesus exhibited a strong gift of discernment. However, Revelations 2:4 reveals to us that God was focusing on the internal motivation of the people and excluded their outward behavior and actions. Jesus says to them, "Nevertheless I have somewhat against thee, because thou hast left thy first love." Notice what it says. God tells the church it left its *first love* and needs to return. That first love was not the work of the ministry - but intimacy with God. The same is true for us. We can find time for everything that comes our way, but fail to seek God's face. Give God some of your time every day. He is most certainly deserving.

{ *In Jeremiah 3:14, God says He is married to the backslider.* }

Here's some exciting news. In Jeremiah 3:14, God says He is married to the backslider. The book of Hosea gives prophetic illustration to this claim. Hosea's relationship exemplifies the love Jesus Christ had for backslidden Israel. The Bible tells us God told Hosea to marry a whore. He was

## Chapter Five - The Process of Repentance

obedient and took a woman name Gomer as his wife. Even though Hosea had her living a more secured life, Gomer still desired to return to the familiar things she used to do and people she used to know. Eventually Gomer left home, and Hosea finds her being sold in the marketplace bound like a slave. She was technically still his wife but somehow she had to be purchased off the auction table. If Hosea wanted her back, he would have to pay whatever it cost to loose her from those chains roped around her neck and tied around her hands and feet. He did just that! He loved her so much that he paid the full price for her redemption.

Gomer was symbolic of Israel and Hosea's love for her is comparable to the love God had for the rebellious nation. Many of us would not have chosen the life Hosea did. If God told us to go marry someone who wasn't our ideal mate, we wouldn't do it. Look at what Hosea went through to show us the power, privilege and essence of repentance. How many of us would have bought Gomer back after she left us high and dry?

In these times, believers are considered to be spiritual Israel, God's people, through the spirit of adoption. Once we accept Christ we are grafted into the covenant God made with Abraham and His descendants. The Bible says of anyone who is of faith [believers], "the same are the children of Abraham" (Galatians 3:7) and that we are "blessed with faithful Abraham" (Galatians 3:9). Abraham lived a life of faith and therefore God justified him and counted his faith as righteousness. Living by faith is simply living a personally intimate, ongoing relationship with God. We, too, must live by faith and not try to live by religious rules and regulations; we are not under the law. It is impossible to fulfill the law. We will break laws. If we break one, we've broken the whole. This is where Christ comes in. He redeemed us from the curse of the law. Furthermore, according to Romans 5:6, Christ showed His unfailing love toward us and died for us when we had nothing within our strength or power to reconcile ourselves back to God. He loved us while we were yet sinners and died for us while we were ungodly. We were nowhere fit to live a kingdom life. But Jesus came and shed His own blood for the remission of our sins. He died that we might repent and come clean and live a life pleasing and acceptable to Him.

Like the story of Hosea and Gomer, how many times has Christ had to buy us back because we wandered off to enjoy the pleasures of sin and backslid in our hearts and eventually our bodies followed? How many times have we gone to the altar and told God with our mouths we would not practice sin anymore, but knew in our minds that we would do it again? Why do we do that? In our hearts we have already left our first love. I'm so thankful to know God is willing to help us even when we get too distracted with the cares of the world.

You can start the process of repentance today. There are three things we must do in accordance with Revelations 2. They are:

## Chapter Five - The Process of Repentance

(1) Remember from where we have fallen,
(2) Repent, and
(3) Do our first works

First, we have to remember. Use your memory to recall all that God has done for you. Verse 5 instructs us to "remember from whence we have fallen." In other words, be honest about the condition of your heart. It is not always easy to admit you have fallen out of love with God. In fact, when we are held accountable for our faults, we tend to become a bit more defensive. In this instance, one might choose to quote a particular Scripture that justifies their imperfection and inclination to sin. After all, the Bible does say, "A righteous man falleth seven times but he gets back up again." Making excuses for your thoughts, actions or repetitive behavior is not acceptable if it is true repentance you're seeking. The Scripture says, "Remember therefore from whence thou art fallen." If you're uncertain whether you have fallen out of love with God, ask yourself the following questions. Is God the first priority in your life? Do you seek Him first before your own desires or needs? Do you spend quality time with Him consistently in prayer, studying the Bible and living a life that is pleasing to Him? If you didn't answer yes to any of those questions, there's a high possibility you have either fallen out of love with The Father or you're on your way to ending your spiritually intimate relationship with God.

The Bible says Jesus rose a great while before day, departed and went to a solitary place (Mark 1:35). Even He thought it was necessary to spend quality time with God. In the book of Revelations, God tells the Church of Ephesus they've fallen out of love with Him.

Listen to what He says next, "Repent." It's the same thing Jesus said! After the Son of God comes up against the devil in the wilderness, the first word Jesus speaks to the people is "repent." Go read it in Matthew. First, while being tempted, Jesus tells the devil, "It is written." However, the first message Jesus delivers to the people is for them to, "Repent; for the kingdom of heaven is at hand." In Revelations 2, when God is talking to the Church at Ephesus, He gives the following instruction: "Remember therefore from whence thou art fallen, and repent." Repentance is the common denominator of what brings us back to Him. In Acts 3:19 Peter said, "Repent, so that your sins will be blotted out when the times of refreshing will come from the presence of the Lord."

This brings me to my next point, Revelations 2:4 not only tells us to remember and repent, but the scripture says, "...and do the first works; or else I will come unto thee quickly, and will remove thy candlestick out of his place, except thou repent." In order to do our first works, we must return to God and remain in His presence. In the text, the

## Chapter Five - The Process of Repentance

people of Ephesus were busy laboring but it wasn't their first work; they had put God on the backburner.

Our first work involves getting in God's presence and sitting at His feet. When we do, He empowers us to be a *mountain dweller*. For instance, Moses would go up on the mountain and spend time with the Lord. Afterwards, he would come down and obey the orders the Lord had given him during his time on the mountain. As many of us return to our first work, we need to realize that God must be included. How can you expect to learn more about God when you leave your bible at church or in the car? When was the last time you texted God? Does he have a ring tone? When your heart is not in tune with God, you'll justify it. We need to be justified, not justifiers. My prayer is that I make it to Heaven. One day our life here on Earth will be over. Where will you spend eternity? The only difference between those who make it to Heaven and those who don't is that the people who obtain eternal life in Heaven will be those who sincerely repented and followed after God.

> *The only difference between those who make it to Heaven and those who don't is that the people who obtain eternal life in Heaven will be those who sincerely repented and followed after God.*

You can teach repentance, you can preach it, but you have to do it. As I reflect back, I praise God for all the adversity and all the things he had to strip me of in order to influence me to come to myself, come clean, and run back to

Him. I understood that I had fallen out of love with Him. The same thing God said in the beginning is the same thing He's saying now – remember, repent and do your first work.

I've told the Lord I will seek His face, primarily because the Scripture tells me to do so. However, what I truly want is God's heart. I understand the requirements of my request. Yet and still some people are seeking God's hand. Why not get to a place where we are like David, a man who was after God's own heart. If I get His heart, I obtain access to the place where everything originates because out of the heart flows the issues of life. I want God's heart.

In order to reach God's heart it is mandatory that we be in close proximity with the Father. For example, the young apostle John had a chance to rest his head on the heart of Jesus Christ. How many of us are after the heart of God? Maybe you need a spiritual heart transplant. Perhaps your spiritual arteries are clogged up and you need surgery to revive those spiritual blood vessels. Jesus Christ blessed us all with the gift of life, so what does it profit us to gain all that stuff we think we want but lose our soul? Think about it.

We've all been in relationships but there is no man or woman who will love you like Christ. The truth of the matter is that you really cannot love your spouse the way you should unless you love them through Christ. When you're in love, you're excited about spending time with that person. You go out of the way to do little sweet things for your spouse. You believe whatever they say because you're in love. But what

## Chapter Five - The Process of Repentance

about God? Is this how you respond to your divine relationship with Him?

Loving God and being in fellowship with Him is not about your convenience. It's not about fitting it in on your "To Do" list. Get God off your agenda and get on His. It's not about what you want; it's about what God wants. You did not create Him, He created you. You don't have to understand everything God's telling you to do, just be obedient to the voice of the Lord.

Sometimes we ask God for things without realizing the distractions that will accompany those things. If our hearts aren't rightly aligned it can be difficult to see how blessed we really are. In a sense we become blind to our blessings and focus solely on what we don't have.

> *The mistake some of us make is that we compare our lives to the lives of other people. We start comparing, competing and complaining. Once an individual reaches this stage, they no longer know who they are and everyone's voice is louder than God's.*

The mistake some of us make is that we compare our lives to the lives of other people. We start comparing, competing and complaining. Once an individual reaches this stage, they no longer know who they are and everyone's voice is louder than God's. It causes us to be frustrated because we walk through life lacking a sense of purpose and direction. Frustration is a sign that you are not hearing God's voice. Even if your circumstances are ideal it doesn't mean you're hearing God's voice. You fail to realize that Satan is the god of this world and he will bless you quick, fast and in a hurry. Our blessing is not in stuff and it's not in positions, it's in God's presence. Get in His presence because that's where we belong.

The presence of God was among God's people, Israel, in the Old Testament in the Holy of holies. Before entrance into the Holy of holies (the presence of God) there was another place where the priest had to come to and minister to God. It was called the holy place. When you look at the holy place, there were three pieces of furniture there. At the center of the holy place (that part of the tabernacle which was also called the inner court) sat the golden altar of incense. It was the highest piece of furniture in the tabernacle and was therefore placed in the center of the room. The golden altar of incense sat higher than the Ark of the Covenant. God commanded the priests to burn incense day and night upon this altar. Incenses were symbolic of prayer or intercession for others, and were considered a sweet fragrance unto God. This tells us that prayer should be at the center of our lives and it should be awarded the highest priority. The Holy Place was positioned between the outer courts and the Holy of Holies.

> *Prayer should be at the center of our lives and it should be awarded the highest priority.*

Prayer should be at the center of every born again believer's life and not the desire to be a billionaire, a best-selling author, an earner of multiple academic degrees or some person of great fame and stature. Prayer should be the center of every believer's focus and careful attention to it may keep us from backsliding, especially since our hearts will be consumed by a constant thirst and need for the presence of God.

CHAPTER SIX

# *The Prize of Repentance*

Throughout the Bible there are several Scriptures that refer to God as our reward or a Rewarder. Repentance is a gift that God is offering to all of us. It is a prize that we can witness through three different promises. God promises to:

(1) Blot out our transgressions,
(2) Never mention our sins again and
(3) Remove our sins from us.

First of all, we repent based on Isaiah 43:25, "I, even I, am he that blotteth out thy transgressions for mine own sake, and will not remember thy sins." The first prize of repentance is that God says He's going to blot out our transgressions. He won't even remember them. Now think about some of the sin you have done. Some of it may have occurred after you were "born again." Isn't it powerful to know that you can confess those things before God, repent for them, and not only will God blot them out but He will not even remember them? Psalm 103:12 tells us, "As far as the east is from the west, so far hath he removed our transgressions from us."

The second prize of repentance is that God will not mention our sin again. This idea is supported by Ezekiel 18:22. God says, "Their transgressions and iniquities I will not mention." God won't even remind you of what you've done. Repentance, combined with the sacrificial death of Jesus Christ on our behalf, makes the removal of our sin possible.

The third prize of repentance is that God says He will remove those same sins from us. This can also be seen in Isaiah 43:25. God says He'll blot out our sins. He'll remove them. But none of this can happen if we never confess our sins. We need to repent for our transgressions and sins, in order to remove them from God's memory and from our past.

Research shows humans are more apt to remember negative experiences versus the positive ones. But in the aforementioned Scriptures, God tells us that if we do not repent, our transgressions will remain and He will remember everything we have ever done. However, repentance is the key that unlocks our freedom from the bondage of sin. If you repent and turn away, you gain God's third promise in regards to repenting.

Not only will God forgive and forget our sins, but He will not remind us of them either. So when we get to heaven,

## Chapter Six - The Prize of Repentance

God cannot bring up anything we repented for that happened during our time here on earth. Too bad the devil does not follow this rule. He is always eager to remind us of our sin. The trick to dealing with the enemy is to expect him to attack and be ready when it happens. The enemy is always living in the past because his past can never be forgiven.

Ironically, the enemy actually understands the power of salvation. However, because his sin was in heaven where he tried to overthrow Christ on His throne, he cannot be saved. Since he knows that he cannot repent of his insurrection, he tries to minimize the importance of repentance to us. The only reason he discredits repentance is because he is not allowed to experience it.

If the tables were turned and the enemy could repent and be forgiven of his sins, I believe he would be the greatest preacher of repentance today. But the devil is jealous of our opportunity to repent so he takes pride in convincing us not to do it either. After all, misery loves company. So, my friend, don't dwell on the negative; don't allow Satan to deceive you. Repent and receive the prize that our great Rewarder has to offer us.

CHAPTER SEVEN

## *Peter's Take on Repentance*

Understanding the Old Testament story of Passover is paramount in its relationship to the teaching of repentance. The story of Passover is initially recorded in the book of Exodus. The Jews have been observing this religious festival ever since the days of Moses. As I stated in chapter five, the Jewish tradition of Passover involves unleavened bread, which is also known as Matzo bread. Matzah bread is square-shaped and contains tiny holes that form horizontal lines. Those holes represent the piercings that Jesus took in his side during crucifixion. The lines represented the stripes (lashes) from the Roman soldier's whip that Jesus received on His body for our healing. The Jews observed the Passover once a year. During that holiday the Jews would take the Matzah bread, divide it, serve one half and store the rest. From one time period to the next, they'd take the Matzah and feed it to anyone who got sick in the house. Before doing so, they'd take the bread, hold it up to God and say, "Lord by faith, you said you'd be our healer." They believed God would heal the person of their illness. Notice the Jews would eat one-half during Passover and kept the rest as a spiritual insurance policy.

For the game the father would play with the children using the Matzah bread, he would break the bread into more than one piece. Then he would send the children outside while he wrapped the other piece in a napkin and hid it somewhere in the house. Whichever child found the hidden piece of Matzo bread would get a gift. However, there was one catch to this prize winning. The winner could not receive their gift until the day of Pentecost.

Now, we also discussed Peter's denial and Judas' betrayal of Jesus. In the midst of all of this, Jesus was arrested, tried, and sentenced to death. Ultimately, Jesus was crucified and took His last breath on that old rugged cross on Golgotha's hill. He died on the cross during Passover. Jesus Christ shed His blood for the remission of our sins during Passover. We know, once Jesus died, His body was resurrected three days later.

I want to include a brief side note about Passover. It is a predominantly Jewish holy day and festival that commemorates the period when ancient Israelites were freed from slavery in Egypt. Passover is one of the most widely observed Jewish holidays.

Now, let's fast forward to Peter's day and time. He, too, observed the Passover. Think back to the day when Jesus'

## Chapter Seven - Peter's Take on Repentance

mother Mary and Mary Magdalene found Jesus' tomb empty. They ran back and told the disciples that Jesus had risen from the dead. Do you remember which disciple went in and found the linen cloths of Christ folded neatly like a napkin? It was Peter! Those neatly folded linen cloths were symbolic of the napkin used in the Jewish tradition of Passover.

When Jesus returns to Peter after the resurrection, He breathes on the disciple and Peter gets reconverted. Because of Peter's denial of Jesus, he fell into an emotional slump. As a result of feeling disloyal and like a failure, Peter went back to what he was familiar with doing – fishing. Peter is the leader, but he told the other disciples he was going fishing. They followed him, unknowingly following a backslidden preacher. If you remember, Peter was on the water the first time he met Jesus. Like Peter, many of us need to repent for reverting back to the lifestyle that we had known before we found Jesus.

As always, Jesus knows where to find us, especially when we feel like giving up or like we failed God. He knew where to find Peter after His resurrection; when Jesus found Peter, he found him so discouraged and disappointed. He was so devastated after seeing his Savior on the cross and so deflated after his denial of Jesus that he went back to find solace in what he used to do; he went fishing. When Jesus found him the first time, Peter had clothes on. The second time, Peter was naked. He was physically and spiritually exposed. It is evident that Jesus is not angry and does not hold a grudge against Peter because He blesses the fishermen with 153 fish.

Afterwards, Jesus questions Peter about his love for Him. It is important to understand the actual translation of words here to get the greatest revelation. If you translate Peter's response, he possesses *phileo* for Jesus. Phileo love is a brotherly love or affection that expects a return. Jesus asks if Peter has *agape* love for Him. Agape love is the highest form of love possible; it is completely unconditional. Peter reiterates his original answer twice more. At this point, Peter repents for denying Jesus, and he admits that his love for Jesus was conditional. Because of Peter's honesty, Jesus extends His mercy toward him and empowered him to strengthen his brethren – the same guys who he led back into the mediocre and mundane chores of just fishing for a couple of shekels each day. Oh what power is demonstrated when God's mercy restores a backsliding preacher! The devil becomes strikingly paranoid when preachers repent!

> *The devil becomes strikingly paranoid when preachers repent!*

Now let me tie the story of Peter together with the Passover. As we refer back to what I mentioned earlier about the Jewish family tradition of using the Matzo bread during Passover, Peter (by seeing Jesus' linen cloth folded into a napkin) is the recipient of the gift. He is the one who received the gift, but he could not get his reward until the

## Chapter Seven - Peter's Take on Repentance

day of Pentecost. On the day of Pentecost, the gift of the Holy Ghost came in that upper room and sat upon everyone there, but it was Peter whom the Holy Ghost used to stand up and preach. The Holy Spirit used this penitent man to preach repentance to the masses – and 3,000 souls came to know Christ from that one message that Peter preached. Repentance will put us in position to receive the gift of the Holy Spirit and cause us to be used mightily by God.

Unlike Peter, Judas dies in his guilt because he failed to repent to God. Peter repented to God and was given another chance to correct his wrong. Peter is symbolic of the church. The Bible says, "Upon this rock I will build my church and the gates of hell shall not prevail against it" (Matthew 16:18). So what is the message here? What God is saying is that if the church repents, He will forgive them. He will give us Jesus' proverbial *napkin* and we will walk away with our Father's gift of eternal life.

Once Peter had come clean of his denial of Jesus and was converted, he was given a gift on the day of Pentecost. He spoke in a new tongue, and it was a visible sign of his being baptized of the Holy Ghost. In Acts 2, we see the power of repentance demonstrated through boldness. Acts 2:14-17a (NIV) reads, "Then Peter stood up with the Eleven, *raised his voice* and addressed the crowd: "Fellow Jews and all of you who live in Jerusalem, let me explain this to you; listen carefully to what I say. These men are not drunk, as you suppose. It's only nine in the morning! No, this is what was spoken by the prophet Joel: In the last days, God says, I will pour out my Spirit on all people..." Peter symbolizes the repentant church and encourages others to walk in boldness and in the newness that accompanies repentance.

Peter begins to share his take on repentance. He stood up boldly and addressed the crowd, "Repent and be baptized, every one of you, in the name of Jesus Christ for the forgiveness of your sins. And you will receive the gift of the Holy Spirit" (Acts 2:38). This is an essential Scripture for the apostolic church. Here Peter tells the people what he has learned through experience and how it has changed his lifestyle. Peter testifies about the validity of repentance. He lets them know that repentance works, not because someone told him but because he experienced it for himself. Peter acknowledges his shortcoming, of how he denied Jesus, and Jesus came back and gave him another chance. Once you have done something and you know it works, it makes you a qualified candidate to tell someone else. Peter tells them to repent for the remission of their sins.

He further tells them that they shall receive the gift of the Holy Ghost. In another place where Peter was preaching after healing a paralyzed man at the temple gate called Beautiful, he gives basically the same message, "Repent, then, and turn to God, so that your sins may be wiped out, that times of refreshing may come from the Lord" (Acts 3:19 NIV).

## Chapter Seven - Peter's Take on Repentance

Notice when you see Jesus, repentance is ushering Him in. Here's Peter (who represents the church) preaching the formula that John the Baptist preached – repentance. Let us not forget, it was John who introduced us to Jesus in the first place. Here, Peter is showing us that same formula - repent and your sins will be blotted out. Throughout the Bible, we see this powerful mystery unfold into the effective formula for conversion.

Another thing I'd like to point out is that the time of refreshing does not come without the sins being blotted out. This blotting out of your sins can only happen as a by-product of repentance. John the Baptist's ministry of repentance introduces us to salvation.

> *The time of refreshing does not come without your sins being blotted out. This blotting out of your sins can only happen as a by-product of repentance.*

The concept of repentance, though originally quite simple, has evolved into such a deep, convoluted mystery. The truth is plain and simple. The church is responsible for preaching the gospel of repentance. Why? The answer is found in John 8:24. Here, Jesus tells the Pharisees and the Jews, "I told you that you would die in your sins; if you do not believe that I am the one I claim to be, you will indeed die in your sins."

Repentance was the preached message of John the Baptist, Jesus, and Peter for the remissions of your sins.

## Coming Clean

There's no way around it. You cannot be reconciled to God without repenting. "Repent, for the kingdom of God is at hand" is my message of hope for you today. So I ask you these three important questions, do you believe that Jesus Christ is who He says He is? Have you repented for your sins? Do you feel remorseful for your wrongdoings? If so you must then ask yourself, are you willing to turn from your sins and dedicated yourself to amending your life and making it ready for the coming of the Lord? Simply asked, "Have you come clean, God's way?"

## About the Author

Anthony Q. Knotts is an entrepreneur, author, motivational speaker, and pastor. The Lexington, NC native is the founding and senior pastor of the Embassy Church International of Greensboro, NC and has been pastoring for twenty years.

True to his entrepreneurial spirit, Anthony Q. Knotts is founder of Manna Systems, LLC, a mobile marketing company, and is CEO of MORE Unlimited, Inc., based on the goal to Motivate Others to Reach Excellence through creating entrepreneurship opportunities and develop holistically (financially, mentally, and spiritually). He is also author of You Can Be M.O.R.E and Liberating the Entrepreneur Within.

Anthony is the proud husband of Byrdzetta Knotts and the father to three wonderful children Teland, Jalen, and Destiny. His life's mission is to learn, to live, and to teach biblical and business principles to help others Be, Do, and Have more in life, in ministry, and in business. He wrote this book as an opportunity for readers to experience coming clean through repentance and to attain the spiritual abundance repentance brings.

www.ingramcontent.com/pod-product-compliance
Lightning Source LLC
Chambersburg PA
CBHW070543300426
44113CB00011B/1770